The beauty of Rose-Marie Sorokin's book *The Miracle of Yes* is that it is comprised of a rich and colourful palette of applicable reflections enticing the reader to contemplate, experiment and practice. The Author draws her inspiration and ideas from some of the most highly regarded Eastern and Western schools of thought, providing a perfect entry point for anybody that seeks to creatively further their possible inner development, to ultimately realise their true potential.

ALEXANDER FILMER-LORCH,
Author of 'The Inner Power of Stillness'
and 'Inside Meditation'

Remembering the soul you came to earth with, nurturing your relationship with it and living in greater harmony with your own soul are some of the most important things you can do with your life. Rose-Marie shares her own journey with great openness and has written The Miracle of Yes to inspire and enable you to do that too.

NICK WILLIAMS,
Author of fifteen books including
'The Work We Were Born To Do'

About the Author

Rose-Marie Sorokin has immersed herself in the fields of yoga, meditation, spirituality, writing and coaching for over 25 years. She teaches classes and YES (Yoga Empowerment Spirituality) weekends in the UK, and hosts retreats in beautiful locations abroad. She also works with people on a one-to-one basis and believes in the power to move from the impossible to the possible, from chaos to peace and from disconnection to Oneness.

Originally from Sweden, Rose-Marie now lives in Kent, UK with her partner with whom she founded Inner Light Yoga & Health Co in 1992.

www.rosemariesorokin.com
www.innerlightyoga.co.uk
www.yogapilatesholidays.com

THE
MIRACLE
OF
YES

RECONNECTING WITH PURPOSE, PASSION
AND PEACE, AND CREATING A LIFE YOU LOVE

ROSE-MARIE SOROKIN

This book is dedicated to the creative source of all life, to the Universe, to the Creator. I wrote it for all those who wish to rediscover their True Self, and who would like to live a life filled with joy and wonder.

Printed in the United Kingdom

First Printing, 2018

Published by Rose-Marie Sorokin Publishing

978-1-9164898-0-6 (print)

978-1-9164898-1-3 (e-book)

The information given in this book should not be treated as a substitute for professional medical advice; always consult a medical practitioner. Any use of information in this book is at the reader's discretion and risk. Neither the author nor the publisher can be held responsible for any loss, claim or damage arising out of the use, or misuse, of the suggestions made, the failure to take medical advice or for any material on third-party websites.

Contents

Acknowledgements

I would like to thank my partner Tim for his continuing love, inspiration and support on this journey. This book would not have been written without him. I would also like to thank my editor Sandy Draper for her wonderful work and help with this book and Drew Jones for the beautiful design. I am also very grateful for all the teachers and authors that have inspired me such as Nick Williams, Mooji, Robert Holden, Louise Hay, Tosha Silver, Teal Swan, Gregg Braden, Davidji, Michael Singer, Adyashanti, Godfrey Devereux, Eckhart Tolle, Alexander Filmer-Lorch and many more.

Introduction

Opening Up to Purpose, Passion and Peace

'Shrug off the no's – they are temporary. This is your world. In your world, there is only yes.'
Jolene Stockman

Life has brought you to this moment. The moment you picked up this book and found your way to this page. There is a part of you that is curious and wants to know more and find new ways of relating to yourself and to the world. Perhaps you've arrived at this point as the result of a difficult experience, such as a divorce, a personal loss or financial challenge. Or perhaps you just have a vague sense that life could be different or you want to find more meaning and create a life that is more in line with your authentic self, that I call the 'True Self'.

Life can be challenging and make huge demands on our time and energy, often resulting in high levels of stress, dissatisfaction and confusion. However, even with small changes you can start moving towards a life you love. This is a decision that *you* make and something that comes from the inside, regardless of your outer circumstances. Just making this decision will shift your energy from 'no' to 'yes' – yes to life and yes to passion, purpose and peace.

This book will take you on a journey of self-development. Somewhere along the line, it's likely that you absorbed the idea that *you are not good enough*. This message, most likely, came from your family, friends, teachers, media or society. If this message is firmly implanted in your subconscious, you may have turned your back on the essence of who you are deep inside and so find yourself moving into experiences of suffering. It is far too easy to get stuck in negative patterns and somehow think that this is normal. It is not.

In the following chapters, I will show you how you can move away from those patterns and into freedom and joy. How you can say 'yes' to your True Self and 'no' to any old, outdated, negative conditioning. Some people will find this transition easy and for others it will be more challenging. But you don't have to do it all in one go. We will take it step by step and you can take as much time as you like on the various chapters and exercises. I recommend that you read the book right through from the beginning to end and do the corresponding exercises, as they have a logical sequence. I also recommend that you start a journal to record your journey so that in time you can look back and see how far you've come.

I have called the exercises 'Reflections', which implies that it is a good idea to take some time for the exercises and allow yourself to become immersed in each one. These practices will help you to:

- Clarify your current situation and understand your thoughts and emotions.
- Understand your negative beliefs, where they come from and how to let them go.
- How to heal and get into the 'yes flow'.
- How to live a heart-based life and develop more self-love and self-acceptance.
- What it means to be awake and inspired, how to meditate and how to develop a spiritual practice.

I have 'road tested' all of these exercises many times with my clients and they have found them to be very useful. For example, on a recent retreat weekend in Kent, one of the participants said, 'Finally someone who tells me what to do and how to do it! I have been to many, many retreats and teachers to try to find an answer, and you have just given it to me. Thank you from my heart.'

You will read more about my work and some of my clients in this book, and how we've managed to turn around our lives with the help of this work. We have all stepped out of fear and into the vastness of possibilities that surround us at all times. Maybe it is time for you too to do the same.

In fact, this book and its title was inspired by the weekend retreats I host on yoga, empowerment and spirituality (YES), and many of the practices have their origins in these weekends but also from my work as a spiritual coach, astrologer and yoga and meditation teacher. It is also a result of decades of my own personal and spiritual development work. As someone who has been teaching yoga and movement for over 30 years I know the importance of working with the body as we store many feelings and emotions in the body tissue. Movement, together with breathing, meditation, spiritual practice and personal development work is powerful and effective. If we can let go of tension on *all* levels of our being we can move forwards very quickly.

By far the biggest source of my inspiration is my clients and retreat participants. I have seen astonishing changes in them in a very short time. It is as if once you give the space and permission for someone to be themselves, they start to flower immediately. I love creating this space of possibilities. People let go of their fears and insecurities and take small or big steps forwards to a new life. I have seen people changing careers, starting businesses, moving home and even country! Starting reading circles, healing groups, meditation groups, going on their dream holiday, meeting a new partner, writing books, becoming artists, becoming speakers/coaches/ spiritual teachers/yoga teachers or just simply saying that they now finally have a stronger self-belief and more confidence. It is when we establish the connection with our True Self that we really start to flourish. When we let go of what other people think, our past and our negative conditioning we are well on our way.

Growing into spirituality

I grew up in a town called Gothenburg on the west coast of Sweden. It is the second largest town in Sweden, after the capital Stockholm. My family was a working-class family and poverty was never far away. There were very few luxuries. My mother made all our clothes, and I learned from her how to make my own and maintain a frugal household. But while we never wanted for anything, my upbringing was marred by sadness, mental health issues and struggle. In the 1960's and 70's this was not something that was talked about, so we lived a 'secret' life and never shared these burdens.

Living with my parents who had both grown up with severe physical, mental and emotional abuse wasn't easy for my brother and I. Of course, they did the best they could but sadly they were scarred for life and never managed to find any degree of peace. This resulted in an atmosphere of sadness and depression at home and I grew up with a lack of real support and encouragement, and I became a shy and inward-looking person. There was always a sense that things were not right and unconsciously I was searching for something better. This degree of emotional drama and hardship at home propelled me into my spiritual journey.

With a very low sense of self-worth I ended up in two difficult relationships. One in my teens and one in my 20's. I eventually managed to end both of these relationships. I didn't realize at the time that I had been deeply traumatized by these experiences and it took many years of healing work to come to terms with this.

Having said this, I also have some beautiful childhood memories, such as the summers we spent in our cottage by the sea. My mother had inherited this cottage and that was our 'luxury'. My talented stepfather built us a boat, which looked distinctly homemade but functioned perfectly, and we spent many happy days exploring deserted islands, making lunch over an open fire and swimming in crystal clear waters. It was during these times, I experienced a sense of freedom and joy, and got in touch with the *real* me. Away from school and the long winters, I spent hours by the sea, thinking, daydreaming, feeding seagulls and foxes from my hand, eating fresh strawberries from our garden and walking deep into the forest to pick wild blueberries. Here I experienced my first taste of a deeper connection with joy, spirituality and my True Self.

So, what is spirituality? For me it is a deep connection with our innermost self (our soul) and with life. It is a connection with the Universal mind and a sense of Oneness with all living things. Of course, when I was a child I hadn't heard of spirituality and it wasn't until much later, when I was in my 20's, that I first encountered this word. The closest thing to spirituality when I was a child was the church. I sensed that there was something of significance there, but couldn't quite connect to it.

Like many other children at that time, I went to Sunday school and was a bit bored by it. What was the point of cutting out figures of Jesus and gluing them onto a piece of paper? Even at this young age I questioned formal religion. However, one evening a week, two nuns in there 60's hosted events. These two nuns were the personification of spirituality and I instantly fell in love with them. They were fun, creative, warm, friendly, patient and full of energy. Even though I was painfully shy, they made sure to include everyone in the group, and I felt loved and at home. We had many evenings of fun, laughter and spiritual discussions – yes, even at this young age. This was what real spirituality was to me. I remember that there was a girl who had the same name as me – Rose-Marie – who became pregnant at 14. She was in the group throughout the whole pregnancy and then with her baby. She was never turned away or looked down on. She was one of us and the nuns made sure of that. They radiated pure love.

These nuns were also friends of my grandmother Anna, and she was a very special person in my life. I had 12 years with her before she passed away, leaving me utterly heart broken. My grandmother had such a lovely energy about her and I loved her dearly. She was my best friend and I fled to her when things got too difficult at home. One of the best things my grandmother knew was when I read the Bible to her. I didn't really have an understanding of what I was reading, but I sensed that there was something sacred about it. We both felt so calm when I was reading, and it was like a deep peace had descended.

My grandmother was also great fun to be with. She liked playing cards, but this was a 'sin' in her church community, and if there was a knock on the door we'd quickly hide the cards. We spent many hours playing cards, talking, laughing and sitting outside in the sun in the summer. I also used to accompany her to church fairs, where there were many stalls where you could buy tickets to win different prizes. My grandmother was known for winning just about everything! She had wonderful winning energies and a good connection to the Divine.

Looking back now at my childhood and early life, I can see how the struggle and hardship made me stronger and more independent. When we are in the middle of a difficult situation we often wonder how we'll survive but somehow, we come out at the other end. Many times, I struggled to see a future, as I was too busy trying to survive for the moment. But life seems to bring us what we need to learn and I came to understand that there is always a Divine guidance.

Saying YES

It has taken me many years to come to the point of writing this book, to step out of my comfort zone and just do it anyway – for myself – and for anyone else who might be interested, and so I simply said 'Yes!'

My life nowadays is very different from my childhood and early years. I have had many experiences that have helped me to move out of sadness and negativity – out of victimhood. Some of these experiences were difficult and some were delightful but all of them had a big impact on me. I realized that I was the 'designer' of my own life and that it was up to me how it would turn out. So, I followed my intuition and started to make changes to my life. For example, in my teens and early 20's I met some wonderful and inspirational people within the worlds of art and dance. I became passionate about both and eventually ended up teaching dance and starting my own dance school. This was in stark contrast to what was considered a normal thing to do at the time. And one day I found a book on astrology - in English. I was hooked! Learning about astrology was a big turning point in my life as I now had a fantastic tool for self-understanding. I remember learning about my own birth chart for the first time and realising that I was unique and that there was nobody else in the whole world that was the same as me. I had permission to be me! What a sense of freedom!

Nowadays I feel that I have a wonderful flow in my life. Yes of course there are challenges even now, but I have a very different foundation to stand on today. I have so much more self-knowledge, self-understanding and self-love these days. I have a solid yoga and meditation practice and a very good spiritual practice. I give myself time to relax and enjoy life. And I am always curious as to what is around the corner. I love the adventure of life!

In the words of Albert Einstein, 'There are only two ways to live your life. One is as though nothing is a miracle. The other is as though everything is a miracle.' And when I stand outside and look at the stars at night I think that it is impossible to *not* be grateful for your life. It is a miracle! The Miracle of Yes!

Chapter 1
Now

'Always say "yes" to the present moment. What could be more futile, more insane, than to create inner resistance to what already is? What could be more insane than to oppose life itself, which is now and always now? Surrender to what is. Say "yes" to life – and see how life suddenly starts working for you rather than against you.'
Eckhart Tolle

When I started saying 'yes', it was the spring of 1990 and I was really struggling. My husband and I had just moved to Kent and I'd quit my job in London due to the long commute. For a while I had to rely on my husband's income to support us until I could get a local job. However, life didn't turn out the way I planned. After years in a difficult marriage, I was finding it increasingly hard to cope, and we finally decided to separate. My husband moved to France and stopped paying his part of the mortgage, leaving me with no income and no way of paying the mortgage or any other bills. It was a very difficult situation to say the least.

I was under huge stress and felt panic-stricken most days, as I realized that I had to find a solution fast. I started to develop a huge fear of what final demand for payment was going to come through the letterbox next. The letters got worse and worse, with threats of legal action, repossession and so on. It was a desperate situation. Apart from writing to the various companies and asking for more time to pay, I was also urgently job hunting but with little success.

One day I felt totally hopeless, in floods of tears, and couldn't see a way out. Sitting there on the floor in my living room, I spontaneously started to pray. Not any kind of religious prayer, but just my own. I explained to the Universe that I needed help, and asked for guidance and assistance. I couldn't see any other way out, so this became a ritual. I would spend one or two hours (often longer) a day, lighting a candle, closing my eyes and praying. I couldn't explain why I was doing this, as I had never really prayed before, but something spurred me on. Something made me take the time to pray. I was desperate, and my intuition told me to do this. In the middle of my chaotic situation, I started to get glimpses of peace and I would experience colours and vibrations as I sat there praying. What I didn't realize at the time was that

I was connecting to my soul and to something much bigger than myself – to the Universe.

That was the start of me saying, 'Yes' to myself, my life, to the Universe and to my future. Before long little miracles started to happen. I got a job, the money started to flow and I began to rebuild my life, and I'll tell you more about this part of my journey later in this book.

The big questions

As Socrates so famously said, 'The unexamined life is not worth living.' And once you start looking at any challenging area in your life, you'll find that many questions arise, such as 'How do I stop worrying?' 'How can I know that things will work out?' 'Why do I feel so alone?' 'How can I feel more love?' 'What is my purpose?' or 'Who am I?' Those were the questions I was asking myself all those years ago and it is the same questions that many of my clients are asking today. This inquiry stage is a vital step on our journey towards more self-understanding and transformation. When we start a process of self-inquiry, it means we are ready to make changes, open ourselves up to new possibilities and new ideas, and we move away from excessive struggle. No matter what your age, this is a good place to be, because this is the starting point of something new. Don't ever think that it is 'too late'. Your life adventure is there for you!

The present situation

I like what Eckhart Tolle said, 'Life will give you whatever experience is most helpful for the evolution of your consciousness. How do you know this is the experience you need? Because this is the experience you are having at the moment.' So often we rush from one thing to another, allowing one day to flow into the next, and never stop for a moment. When I teach my yoga classes, I create a space for everyone to stop and just be present in the moment; this is mindfulness in action and it is the same with a meditation practice; it provides a space to be still and to stop, breathe and relax. It is a great idea to schedule some of these moments into your day and week, and we'll explore this more through the book.

A good place to start your journey towards inner peace is this exercise. It is a quick evaluation of where you are right now in your life and an opportunity to land in the present moment.

Reflection: The present situation

This exercise has three steps and will help you to become more aware of your present situation.

Step 1

Have a pen and your journal ready. Take a moment right now and be still. Close your eyes. Take a few deep breaths. Ask yourself:
- Where am I now?
- Who am I now?
- What is going on in my life right now?

And then write down what comes to mind. Here follows how two of my clients answered:

Examples:

Jane: 'I am 43, married with two children and work as a solicitor. I enjoy my job, but suffer from feeling overwhelmed from time to time. I wish I could have more time with the children. I am a little confused about the future. I long to express myself more, maybe as a writer. Generally, I have a good life, with a good income and a nice home, but I suspect that there's a lot more to life than what I am experiencing right now.'

Peter: 'I am 60 and have just retired. I've been running a successful business for many years and just sold it. I am married with three grown-up boys. At the moment I feel very lost, as I'm used to being busy and now have nothing to do all day, and am unsure what to do or which direction to go.'

You have just put down on paper a little about your current thoughts and circumstances. Maybe this was the first time you have done this. This is a good starting point, and will give you some ideas and clarity about your present life. Let's take it to the next step.

Step 2

Again, just take a moment and close your eyes. Take a few deep breaths. Ask yourself:
- What are my *feelings* about my current situation?

Focus on your heart area, and ask yourself what you are feeling when you think about your current circumstances. There is no right or wrong here:

Examples:

Jane: 'I generally feel OK, but I can also feel sadness in my heart. I am not sure why.'

Peter: 'It feels strange. Empty. I feel a little fearful. I am telling myself to pull myself together.'

Step 3

Stay with this feeling for a moment. Try to relax into it. Feel the feeling. Ask yourself:

- What message does this feeling have?
- What does it want to tell me?

Write it down. Again, there are no right or wrong answers.

Examples:

Jane: 'I think it wants to tell me that I need to create more space in my life for enjoyment and relaxation. Maybe it's telling me that I am rushing around too much and need to slow down.'

Peter: 'Strange, because in the middle of this emptiness I can feel a seed of joy! I actually have some more time to myself now. What comes to mind is that I should take up painting and drawing again.'

I used this three-step process as part of my healing process to help me accept what was going on at the moment and realize that things would improve. I also realized that I hadn't listened to my intuition for a very long time. That was a clear message for me at that point.

Stop and listen

It can be very useful to stop, breathe and listen inwards from time to time to find out where you are right now and just relax into the present moment – regardless of what you feel and what is going on in your life right now. Eckhart Tolle says that 'feeling will get you closer to the truth of who you are than thinking'. By taking these moments of looking inwards and spending time in stillness, we get to know ourselves better, and this is also the way to self-acceptance and acceptance of the present. We stop wanting to run away from *what is* and thereby create more peace within ourselves.

To help you understand what acceptance means think of the ocean. Your thoughts, feelings and sensations are the waves of the ocean – coming and going. There are big strong waves and there are soft gentle waves; they are all water and all part of the ocean. At the deepest level of the ocean there is stillness. You are the ocean – all parts of it. You know that you have a vast stillness and peace within yourself, and that the waves are on the surface. You accept the waves as a part of you. None of the waves can harm or destroy you, as you have this deep peace within you. The ocean and the waves are inseparable.

The choices we make

Wherever you are in your life, you got there by making lots of different choices – some good and some not so good. Some were conscious and some unconscious. In my case, I made many different choices to get to where I was in 1990. For example, I had chosen to move abroad and thereby leave my home country, family and friends, get married, buy a house that needed a lot of work, change career, etc. Some of these choices seemed wonderful at the time, but others caused me grief and sadness. However, with awareness I started to make better choices. I learned to focus on what I really wanted and to listen to my intuition, instead of rushing into situations. However, when I look at the larger picture of my life, I realize that I was *meant* to make all these choices, and they have taken me to where and who I am today. I am grateful for that journey.

I believe that we are all responsible for our choices. It is easy to blame it on our individual circumstances, parents, partners, the economy, our health etc., but the fact is that somewhere along the line you made several different decisions that took you in a certain direction. Some people have difficulties accepting this, and I can understand that. It can feel very hard to accept that we are responsible for our current situation (I really struggled with this at first!). However, if you can accept where you are right now and relax a little, you can also change it and move on. You can make other choices.

Your choice

Is it time for you to make other choices and take a different direction in life? Do you want a life that is a more accurate reflection of who you really are? If you are willing to step out of the comfort zone and make different choices, you may be on a journey of adventure and excitement (and some challenging bits too!). You may find new groups of people that are more on your wave length and you may have a dramatically increased sense of inner peace. You will know what it is like to live a life you love, and stop living a life according to other people's views and opinions. You are ready to heal your life, move on and embrace a new future. You are ready to say 'Yes!' Once you start to heal, it will have a dramatic effect on yourself, other people and the planet because you are so much more powerful than you realise.

Reflection: 10 deep breaths

Use this simple exercise anytime you need to feel more present and peaceful.

Get into a comfortable position and make sure you won't be disturbed. Close your eyes.

1. Place your hands on your abdomen around the navel area.
2. Take 10 deep breaths. Feel the abdomen move under your hands. As you breathe in, the abdomen gently expands. As you breathe out, it sinks back down. You can imagine a balloon inflating as you breathe in and deflating as you breathe out. Keep the breath steady and relaxed.
3. Then take a moment and notice how you feel.

Chapter 2

Thoughts

'We are what we think. All that we are arises with our thoughts. With our thoughts we make the world.'
Buddha

From an esoteric and quantum physics viewpoint, our thoughts, feelings, beliefs and intentions effect our energy field. Science discovered that there is a huge unified universal energy field and we are all in this field together. In 1944, Max Plank identified the existence of this unified field and called it 'the Matrix'. He believed that, underlying everything we can see, our bodies included, there's an intelligent and conscious mind. Gregg Braden calls this 'the Divine Matrix'. Others call it 'God' or the 'Universal Mind'.

Our individual energy fields are constantly interacting with each other and with this vast universal energy field. Our thoughts and feelings are shaping and influencing our energy field, each and every moment of our lives, and the energy we radiate effects *what we* experience. Our individual energy field is constantly communicating with everything around us. Perhaps this puts in perspective just how incredibly powerful our thoughts, feelings, beliefs and intentions are!

For example, if we carry a large amount of negative emotions and traumatic memories in our energy field, this may have an impact on our daily life. We may have low self-esteem and be hesitant to take initiatives and to stand up for ourselves. We may make choices that are not in our best interest. We may have difficult relationships as the people in our lives are reflecting back to us our inner turmoil.

On the other hand, having a predominantly positive outlook and generally feeling good about ourselves it is much more likely that we will have positive experiences in life. We might be better at listening to our intuition and make better choices. Our relationships might be more fulfilling as they will reflect our positive outlook back to us.

We are constantly creating our reality – positive or negative or somewhere in-between.

The inside is more important than the outside

When I discovered that there was a limit to what I could change on the outside, I started to go within. When you come to the realization that what goes on inside of you is the most important thing in your life, you have what is often referred to as an 'awakening'. There isn't really anything on the outside, because everything on the outside, so to speak, is a result of what is going on inside. Your thoughts, attitudes, feelings and beliefs are reflected outwards in the form of your experiences, relationships and events. It is all one energy.

For example, have you noticed that when you are stressed, other things seem to go wrong too? This is due to acting from a place of disharmony. Your inner mental or emotional state is out of balance, and the result is that this is reflected outwards in the form of stressful or challenging experiences. On the other hand, if you're feeling calm inside, things seem to go well. Your day flows well, you have good conversations with people around you and you may discover something fun or interesting.

Of course, this may not *always* be the case. You can feel stressed and things still work out OK. It is when the stress and the negativity have reached a critical point that it starts to affect your life and your circumstances more seriously. We are designed to be able to handle a certain amount of stress, difficulties and challenges, and most of us are able to work things out and move back into a more positive and relaxed state. However, it is when we are suffering from long-term stress, or even trauma, that this can dominate our life and result in negative experiences, such as health problems, relationship problems, depression and things just generally not working out so well.

So, whether you're aware of it or not, your power to think, feel and imagine is working all the time. We are constantly visualizing, or seeing things, in our mind's eye, and those thoughts and images are the first step in what we create in our lives, just like an architect first has a thought about how they want a building to look and then makes it a reality. However, it can be a bit of a challenge to become aware of our own thought patterns, but once we become aware we can also start changing them.

Who's talking?

It is estimated that the human brain processes between 50,000–70,000 thoughts per day. There is always something going on in the mind, and unfortunately most of those thoughts are repetitive, dwelling in the past, fearful of the future or simply utter nonsense. How many of these thoughts do you think you are aware of?

Most of the repetitive thoughts are on automatic – programmed into the subconscious mind and beyond our conscious awareness. And did you know that the conscious mind can process about 40 bits of information per second, but the subconscious mind can process 40 million bits of information per second!

Given the huge number of thoughts and the incredible power of the subconscious, you might be wondering whether we are ever in control? But I don't think we need to control our thoughts, just have what I call a 'mental gate', so that negativity doesn't seep into our subconscious based on previous thought patterns and experiences.

We'll talk more about how beliefs are formed in the next chapter. For now, it's just important to understand that most of our negative thoughts are programmed in childhood and those thoughts went straight into our subconscious minds – unquestioned and unchallenged. These thoughts and beliefs most likely came from our parents, teachers or other adults, and as children we easily absorb them and they become *our* thoughts. Over time, these thoughts can turn into negative beliefs, such as 'I am not good enough' or 'the world is a dangerous place' and trigger emotional responses that, before we can process what has happened, overwhelm us. Thoughts either support us or they don't. Some can be helpful and effective. Others can be limiting, negative and harmful, and a lot of thoughts can be just mental noise, nothing important.

Thoughts – going back in time

Let's go back in time. The modern human mind, with its amazing ability to analyse, plan, create and communicate has largely evolved over the last 100,000 years. All those years ago, the mind had one major and important function – to help us survive in a world full of danger. Imagine that you are one of those early human beings. What are your most important needs in order to survive and reproduce? They are food, water, shelter and reproduction. So, your priority is to look out for danger and avoid it. The main priority for primitive humans was to stay alive as long as possible and, with each generation, we became more skilled at avoiding danger.

Today the mind is functioning in a similar way. It is constantly assessing environments that it encounters – Is it good or bad? Safe or dangerous? Harmful or helpful? However, these days it is not a wolf or tiger that we encounter but the situation of losing our job, being rejected, embarrassing ourselves in public, getting a serious illness, or many other common worries. As a result, we tend to spend a lot of time worrying about scenarios that, more often than not, never happen.

Another important aspect of survival for early humans was to belong to a group. If your tribe rejects you, it won't be long before some dangerous animal finds you. So how does the mind protect you from rejection by the tribe? By comparing you with other members of the clan: Am I fitting in? Am I doing the right thing? Am I contributing enough? Am I as good as the others? Does this sound familiar?

Our modern-day minds are constantly warning us of rejection and comparing us to the rest of society. No wonder we spend so much energy worrying about whether people will like us. No wonder we're always looking for ways to improve ourselves or putting ourselves down because we don't 'measure up'. In the distant past, we only had a small group of people to compare ourselves to, but nowadays we have newspapers, magazines, advertising, TV and social media. We are bombarded with images of seemingly 'perfect' people and we compare ourselves to them. We are constantly comparing, evaluating and criticizing ourselves, and focusing on what we think we are lacking. No wonder we find it so difficult to be happy and find inner peace.

Thoughts – the science bit

Neuroplasticity is the science that looks at how our brain is being reshaped by our thoughts. Norman Doidge, MD, psychiatrist, psychoanalyst and author of *The Brain That Changes Itself* (2007) says that our brain is capable of changing for our entire lives. When we learn something new, the old neural pathways are overlaid with new ones. This creates new patterns of thought and behaviour.

The brain contains a network of synapses, each one separated by an empty space called a 'synaptic cleft'. Whenever you have a thought, one synapse sends a chemical across the cleft to another synapse, and thereby building a bridge over which an electrical signal can cross, carrying along its charge of the information you're thinking about.

Every time this electrical charge is triggered, the synapses grow closer together, in order to decrease the distance that the electrical charge has to cross; this is called 'adaptation'. The brain is rewiring its own circuitry, physically changing itself, to make it easier for the thought to trigger. So therefore, your thoughts reshape your brain. Isn't that amazing?

So, if your persistent thoughts are those of fear, regret, disappointment or anger, these will be *reinforced* in your brain. And it is the same thing with thoughts of love, optimism or inspiration – they will also be reinforced.

So, it's worth asking yourself:
- What kind of thoughts do you predominantly want to think?
- How do you want to shape your brain, thought processes and your future?

Dealing with negative thoughts

We'll explore meditation in more depth in Chapter 9, but mindfulness is a great way of working with negative thoughts, depression and anxiety. Here are a few things you can do:

25

- **Imagine how young children and animals act in the world**: They are connected to what is going on in the present. Try to bring a gentle curiosity to life, just as animals and children do. When we approach our thoughts in this way, we are more relaxed and don't feel such a strong need to label them as good or bad. Instead, we just explore them, with a childlike wonder, and let them be nothing more than what they are – thoughts.
- **Practise yoga — especially the slightly harder poses**: Yoga is a form of moving meditation. When we practise yoga, we become more anchored in the present, as our awareness is focused on what is happening within the body. It is particularly useful to focus on more challenging poses such as downward-facing dog, plank or warrior 1, and to be aware of any sensations and even some slight discomfort. Try to embrace each pose, be present and breathe through it. When we feel depressed or anxious, it sometimes feels like it will never end but practising challenging yoga poses teaches us to accept the challenge and to trust that, just like anything else, it will pass.
- **Take a mindful shower**: All the activities that we perform on a daily basis, such as showering, often become the most mindless, because we do them on automatic pilot. The next time you are in the shower, focus on the sensation of the water on your skin. Notice the temperature. How is the pressure? Be aware of the scent of your shampoo or body wash. Really bring yourself into the moment and actually think about what you are doing. Notice how this experience differs from your usual routine.
- **Use your hands**: Make something with your hands. Activities such as painting, sewing, pottery, baking, photography, DIY, gardening, colouring or anything practical can be incredible soothing, rewarding and help you to create more inner peace.
- **Get out in nature**: Go for a solitary walk in nature and really look at what you can see, such as the trees, plants, flowers and sky. This activity is best done on your own so you can really focus on your experience.

If you feel negative, depressed and anxious, remember to be patient and loving with yourself. We all have moments of sadness and negativity. It is important to accept what is but eventually move on.

Becoming aware of your thoughts

One of the most common questions I am asked by students and clients is 'How can I become more aware of my thoughts?' As we discovered in the previous section on neuroplasticity, what we think about, and focus on, shapes our lives. Marianne Williamson says, 'You must learn a new way to *think* before you can master a new way to *be*.' With an awareness of our thoughts, we can also change them for more positive ones and enjoy the results.

Reflection: The two assistants

Use the following exercise to help you become more aware of your thoughts and practice using the 'mental gate' to help you stop unhelpful and negative thoughts from becoming negative feelings and beliefs. Imagine that you have two assistants, one sitting on your right shoulder and the other on your left shoulder. They are your thinking assistants.

Supporter: On the right-hand side sits a character that's friendly and supportive.

Inner Critic: On the left-hand side sits a character that is critical and negative but not really evil; they just don't know any better.

When a thought comes through, listen and see which side is telling you this. Is it the Supporter or the Inner Critic? Is it helpful, negative or just nonsense? This is where you start to notice. You become more aware of your thoughts. The process gets better with practice.

Filtering thoughts: If the thought is just nonsense, imagine that one (or both) of your assistants are throwing it away.

When a negative thought comes through do the following.

Have a conversation with your assistants: Say 'Is that true?' 'Why do you say that?'. Then listen and see what your Inner Critic is saying. Maybe your Supporter also has something to say.

Take some notes in your journal of anything you learned from doing this exercise.

Who's thinking?

We tend to be very identified with our thoughts. We may ask ourselves - Who is talking in my head? Rumi says 'Out beyond ideas of right-doing and wrong-doing, there is a field. I'll meet you there.' We are so much more than our thoughts, and we need to let go of the over-identification with what is going on in our head. We need to let go of the frazzled mind and allow our heart to speak.

One of the most consistent themes among many wisdom traditions is the teaching, 'The truth shall set you free'. However, in the West we tend to believe that the truth is a mental or verbal story, a set of words. Many Eastern traditions teach that words are 'pointers' to the truth. The words themselves are not the truth. Truth is something you *live*, not something you think.

Reflection: Negative thoughts and their opposites

- In your journal, make a list of five thoughts that tend to pop up in your mind and bother you. Thoughts that cause you worry, anger or sadness.
- Now think of a way that the opposite of each thought could also be true. You mind will probably immediately reject this but keep going and see what happens.

Examples:

Anne, one of my clients, had the repetitive thought 'I am not lovable, and nobody wants me'. The opposite would be 'I am lovable and desirable'. At first, Anne just didn't think that this was true, but after having reflected on it she realized that she was loved – by her children, by her parents, friends and many other people. The thought 'I am not lovable, and nobody wants me' wasn't true.

Catherine's persistent thought was 'I am ugly' and the opposite 'I am beautiful' didn't go down well with her! At first, she just couldn't see that this was true. But when we talked about this, it turned out that several people throughout her life had told her that she was beautiful, and she even had a 'secret' admirer at work!

Now write down your five opposing thoughts in your journal. Take a moment and reflect on these thoughts. Be kind to yourself.

Chapter 3
Beliefs

'Our beliefs are creating our reality.'
Joe Vitale

Many of the things that you were told as a child have turned into beliefs. A belief is a thought that has been repeated many, many times and eventually turned into a belief. Some beliefs are good and useful, such as being organized and tidy or polite and some are negative and even harmful. Our beliefs help us provide stability in our lives by compartmentalizing everything in order to make sense of the world. So, as you go through life, you form habits, beliefs and values, and you have experiences that form memories that are stored in the unconscious mind. These beliefs, values and habits are determined by your culture, parents, peers, teachers, TV, social media, music, books, politics, as well as assumptions and misunderstandings.

Once we have a belief, any information from these sources is filtered so that we strengthen our original belief and reject any information that may contradict it. For example, if someone believes they are ugly or stupid, then no amount of reassurance from friends or family can help them believe otherwise, as they reject any information that contradicts their belief.

When a belief is repeated over and over again, it is strengthened. Before the age of five, we basically take everything in without question, because we have nothing to compare it to. As we get older, our 'filter' becomes stronger so that less and less suggestions are allowed in. By the age of 12 our main belief system is largely set in place, but of course it can still be influenced. The key is to become *aware of your beliefs*, where they come from and what impact they have on your life. You can then start working on replacing any self-limiting or negative beliefs.

So, what do you believe? One of the most important steps to changing our beliefs is to discover what we actually believe.

The reality of our day-to-day experience is a reflection of our thoughts and beliefs. If you are unhappy in any area of your life, you need to look at what beliefs you have in that area. For example, if you keep thinking a thought like *I am stupid* (and have a belief of inferiority), a manifestation of that thought might be that you keep failing exams or you don't start the business you have always dreamt about. What is it that makes you experience similar negative situations again and again? It isn't actually the people, circumstances and events in your life that are causing you to be unhappy. It is the thoughts and beliefs *about* the people, circumstances and events that are making you unhappy.

We often believe that things *should* be different to what they are or were. This is a resistance to the now or the past. It is difficult to feel inner peace if we hang on to this resistance. Some examples of common core challenges and associated fears or self-limiting beliefs include:

- **Abandonment:** Nobody cares about me. I'm all alone. I don't matter. I can't trust anyone.
- **Arrogance:** I'm better than all of you. I'm right and you're wrong.
- **Damaged:** Something is wrong with me. I'm a failure. I'm damaged.
- **Inferiority:** I'm not good enough. I'm stupid. I'm worthless. I'm boring. I'm hopeless.
- **Rejection:** I'm a burden. I'm unwanted. Nobody wants to spend time with me.
- **Shame:** I'm bad. I'm evil. I'm a mistake. I'm a monster. I'm disgusting. I'm possessed.

One of my clients, Elizabeth, attended one of my YES weekends and when we came to define what it is that we really want in life, she wrote down that she had always dreamed of having a house by the sea.

'That sounds wonderful,' I said.

'But it won't happen,' she said.

'Why do you say that,' I asked.

'Because I just know. It won't happen. It will never happen.'

We had a discussion around this, and it was challenging! She had real difficulties in seeing that she was blocking her own success by thinking self-limiting thoughts. What core belief was behind these thoughts? That she didn't deserve. Deep down she didn't believe that she deserved success, happiness and any other good things in her life. She had a long-term core belief of being non-deserving and not good enough.

Reflection: Core limiting beliefs

- Look at the Five Negative Thoughts that you wrote down earlier. By reading them, can you figure out what your most dominant Core Negative Belief is? Make a note of it in your journal.

Sometimes when you do this exercise the core limiting belief that you come up with may sound totally crazy, and you didn't even realize that you had it, but that is often because it has been covered up for such a long time and is mainly operating in your subconscious. When you become aware of your core limiting beliefs, then you can do something about them.

Changing your core limiting beliefs

So how do you change your beliefs? The first step is to become aware of them (for example by doing the exercise above) and then simply letting them go. Realize these core limiting beliefs are not true but based on somebody else's opinions, values and beliefs, and that you have been carrying around in your subconscious since childhood. A core negative belief is not who you really are; it is not your True Self. And it is definitely time to say goodbye to all those self-limiting and negative beliefs and move forwards in life.

Reflection: Source of your beliefs

Now that you have become aware of your core negative beliefs, this exercise will help you to understand where they come from.
Draw a simple table like the one shown below in your journal. Now go back to your most dominant core negative belief(s) and make a note of it and where each one comes from.
For example:

Core negative belief	Where does it come from?
I can't trust anyone – abandonment	Being taken into care as a child because your parents couldn't cope (due to mental illness, drug abuse etc.)
I am not good enough – inferiority	You were told by your parents/ teachers/caretakers that you were not clever/beautiful/funny.

Now ask yourself the following questions and make a note of your answers in your journal:
- Are your core limiting beliefs true?
- Are they *really* true?
- Can you see where your core beliefs are coming from?
- Can you see that they are coming from other people?

31

- Do you understand that you no longer need to believe them?
- Can you let go of them?

You may come to the conclusion that your negative core beliefs are simply not true. They come from when you were a child and were inherited from your caretakers/parents/teachers, etc. It is time to let them go and to take your power back. By letting go of your negative core beliefs you are getting to know your True Self.

Reflection: Healing limiting beliefs

I have used this exercise myself in the past and now use it with my groups, and it can help you to further let go of your limiting beliefs. Take a moment to get still. Close your eyes and relax.

1. Place your right hand (not just the fingers) on the upper chest over your heart.
2. Begin to rub your upper chest soothingly in a clockwise circle around the sternum, including over your heart.
3. As you continue rubbing, begin to repeat aloud or silently:
   - 'I deeply love and accept myself, even though I have believed I am powerless.'
   - 'I deeply love and accept myself, even though I have held this belief for a long time.'
   - 'I deeply love and accept myself, as I choose to let this old limiting belief go.'

How long have you been saying no?

Coming down to the nitty gritty of life – we are either saying YES or NO to life.

Almost all of us, including me, have been saying NO most of our lives. Take your age and subtract five. It is likely that you have been saying NO to yourself for that length of time. When we are infants our whole being is about saying YES, with a big smile and open arms, exploring and playing, having fun. However, as we grew up we learned how to say NO. No to being ourselves, no to believing in ourselves, no to our passion, no to our talents, no to our feelings, no to our creativity, no to our 'crazy' ideas, no to adventure, no to experimenting, no to having 'too much' fun, no to being too loud or too quiet, no to living fully and completely.

Why? Because our parents and/or carers, teachers and other people around us said no to all these things in their own life, and were brought up in the same way. They transferred their self-limiting beliefs to us. Comments such as,

- 'Don't be so stupid.'
- 'Who do you think you are?'
- 'Control yourself',
- 'You are giving me a headache.'
- 'I won't love you anymore, if you do that.'
- 'You are an idiot!'
- 'You can't do anything right.'
- 'You are so messy.'
- 'I am never going to speak to you again.'
- 'Stop acting like a baby' or 'Don't cry!'
- 'Stop bothering me.'
- 'Be a good girl/boy for Mummy/Daddy.'

We often heard these and similar messages repeated.

How can we grow up to be balanced, harmonious, confident, happy and creative people with those messages drummed into us? If comments like these are repeated over and over again they form the belief that 'we are not good enough' or that there is 'something wrong with us'. The feeling is that we don't fit in and that we are not loved or accepted the way we are. Luckily more parents have more awareness these days and can avoid using these undermining comments.

If, however, we have grown up with these types of messages, we then develop what is sometimes called an 'approval addiction'. We quickly learn that if our parents or other grown-ups are pleased with our behaviour, we will be loved. If they were not, the love would be withdrawn, and we would maybe even be punished. So, we modify our behaviour accordingly.

We are trained to be more concerned with approval than anything else. We learn to change our behaviour so that we can receive love. In the process, we often suppress feelings, as we know that certain feelings are not OK. It could for example be the case that your parents have difficulties dealing with their own feelings of fear, sadness and anger and therefore suppress them and you learn by their example. If you express such feelings, you may get the message that you are a 'bad person'.

- 'Good girls/boys don't get angry.'
- 'Control yourself!'
- 'Behave!'
- 'Get over it.'
- 'Enough.'
- 'That's ridiculous! How can you be upset/angry about *that*?'

There is also a cultural aspect to this 'approval addition'. For example, in my home country of Sweden, we even have a specific word for this. We call it *jantelagen* – the 'law of not standing out'. It is ingrained in us, from a very early age that it is not a good idea to 'stand out', be different from other people, be too loud or too ambitious.

Who is saying no?

One of my clients, Susan, was a project manager at a large company in London. She had a good job and salary, but she hated her job. She was in tears when we spoke. She felt trapped and exhausted. She was working long hours, much longer than was expected of her, but she felt that she needed to do that to be appreciated and respected. 'They don't respect me,' she said, and 'I need to show them that I am good at my work.'

There are two parts to yourself, we can call them the 'Conditioned Self' and the 'True Self', which I spoke of earlier. Your True Self formed before you were born and will stay with you your whole life. This is who you really are, the real or authentic you. This is the essence of who you are and represents your dreams, passions and desires or what makes you feel joy, peace and happiness.

Your beliefs can also be called the Conditioned Self, which formed as you grew up in response to influences from people around you, including everyone in your family, friends, teachers etc. Your Conditioned Self has picked up a huge variety of skills, such as talking, reading, writing, driving, cooking and behaving appropriately but also a lot of negative beliefs. This part of you was formed by cultural norms and expectations. For example, if you were born into a family of drug dealers you may be wary, street-smart and ruthless. If you were raised by nuns, you may be saintly and self-sacrificing. Your Conditioned Self is hard at work, right now, to 'get things right', whether that is to be reliable and hard-working, cute and sexy or tough and macho. Anything that makes you socially acceptable. It is a form of approval addiction we talked about earlier.

For most of us, these two parts of ourselves are in battle with each other. There is an internal conflict between the Conditioned Self and the True Self. Unfortunately, most of the time it is the True Self that is losing out. That could be the case for you right now, or you may not have picked up this book. Look at the table below to understand the differences between the Conditioned Self and the True Self:

Conditioned Self	True Self
Avoidance	Inspired
Conforming	Unique
Imitating others	Inventive
Predictable	Spontaneous
Overworking	Playful
Fearful	Loving
Competing	Cooperating
Lonely	Whole

Coming back to Susan, she had almost completely suppressed her True Self, and had allowed her Conditioned Self to rule her life. She did what others were expecting of her (or at least that is what she thought they were expecting) and overruled her exhaustion and unhappiness. Her True Self was screaming at her to stop and listen inwardly.

Reflection: Part 1 – What are you saying no to?

Have a pen and your journal ready. Take a moment right now and be still. Close your eyes. Take a few deep breaths. Now ask yourself:

- What areas in my life don't I like?
- What qualities in myself do I have difficulty accepting?
- What things or areas in my life don't feel good?
- What am I saying NO to in my life?

And then write down what comes to mind. Don't think for too long, just spontaneously write down what comes up.

Examples:

Bridget: 'I have trouble accepting my body – I am saying NO to my body. I am struggling with my health and weight. I also don't like being 62 and getting old. I am saying NO to age and life.'

Zoe: 'I have a hard time hiding my anxiety at work. I suffer with panic attacks from time to time and I hate it! I don't know what to do about it. I am saying NO to my feelings. I am also nervous about my job, as there is a risk of redundancy. The strange thing is, I don't think I even like my job, but I have never said this to anyone. I am saying NO to being honest with myself about my job.'

Joe: 'I have never felt that I can live up to the male ideal. You are supposed to be tall and muscular and I have never been that! I think that this has had an impact on my relationships, and I have difficulties finding the right partner. I have several failed relationships behind me. I am lacking in confidence. I am saying NO to me and to who I am.'

Reflection: Part 2 – What are your feelings about this?

What are your feelings about this? Again, just take a moment and close your eyes. Take a few deep breaths. Focus on your heart area, and ask yourself what you are feeling when you think about the things you just wrote down.

Examples:

Bridget: 'Oh gosh I feel a lot of fear! But I am also happy that I am looking at this!'

Zoe: 'Anxious. And at the same time there is a kind of hope.'

Joe: 'Lonely. Like nobody loves me.'

Whatever your response, stay with this feeling for a moment. Try to relax into it. Feel the feeling.

What message does this feeling have? What does it want to tell you? Write it down.

Examples:

Bridget: 'I need to let go of all this fear, because it doesn't help me at all. I need to work on accepting myself and my body. I also need to look at why I am eating so much unhealthy food.'

Zoe: 'I want to learn some breathing techniques to calm down and control my anxiety. I also need some help with finding out why I am so anxious. I think I need to look for another job.'

Joe: 'It is OK to be lonely from time to time. And it is not actually true that nobody loves me.'

It is good to be totally honest with yourself. Often, we silently hope that our 'bad' sides (our 'shadow') such as procrastination, overspending, overeating, criticizing, etc. should just go away. Yet, often nothing happens. We carry on with our work, raising our children, chasing success and suffer in silence. We 'forget' about our dreams and passions, and just focus on surviving. We think 'maybe things will be better next year'.

The term 'shadow' was first used by the psychotherapist Carl G Jung to describe the denied or repressed part of ourselves. By acknowledging these repressed aspects of ourselves, we free up a lot of energy. This makes is much easier to move ahead in life. See Chapter 4 for more on the 'shadow'.

Reflection: Five things that you would like to change

- In your journal, make a list of five things that you would like to change in your life. The previous exercise may have given you a few clues.

You have now identified a few things that you would like to improve or change in your life. Well done! We will come back to this later in the book.

Chapter 4
Feelings and Emotions

'We must go within to heal.'
Louise Hay

I have lost count of how many times I have asked a client what they are feeling and just had a blank response. Unfortunately, most people are out of touch with their feelings. They may exist in a bland pleasantness or maybe even in a depressed state, hiding their strong emotions. One way of getting in touch with your feelings and emotions is to work with your body. Your body never lies.

We tend to have a difficult relationship with our body. Often there is a kind of war going on. The body gets sick, it doesn't look or behave the way we want it to, and it doesn't live up to the ideals presented by the media. We therefore often disassociate ourselves from our body and develop what is called 'disembodiment'. We feel out of touch with our body, our emotions and our sense perceptions. Most of us spend our lives with very little actual awareness of our body. We are obviously aware that we have a body, but we are thinking about the body rather than feeling it, and we may think about our body in an apprehensive or even self-destructive way. We have thoughts about the body but very little direct experience of the body itself.

Examples of our modern disembodiment are how so many people continually want to 'look better', obsessing about body shape, dieting, exercise, make up and clothes. Or how we ignore the body when it is sick and keep pushing on even though we need to rest and recover. We may develop addictions to food, antidepressants, drugs or alcohol. And much of this is because we find it too difficult to stop for a moment and simply *feel*.

Although everything may seem fine with us from the outside, inwardly these experiences, just in and of themselves, can plunge us into a personal crisis. We feel lost. Perhaps without even knowing exactly what is wrong, we begin looking for ways back into our body and our life.

Embodiment

The body has its own beautiful wisdom, all you have to do is to listen to it. Today we are experiencing an increasing inability to experience our own emotional life with any degree of openness, trust or confidence. Emotions are arising out of the darkness of the body, they are felt intensely, and call us back into the body. We need to be unconditionally present to our own emotions and not separate ourselves from them and withdraw into judgements or self-loathing.

Our lives are often packed full of things to do and there seems to be very little time for the unexpected. We often think that we have had a successful day when we have managed to accomplish all the things on our 'to do' list. Emotions however have no timetable. Psychotherapist, teacher and author John Welwood says:

> *Emotions are our most common experience of being*
> *taken over by forces seemingly beyond our control.*
> *Usually, we regard them as a threat, imagining that if*
> *we really let ourselves feel our anger or depression, they*
> *would totally overwhelm us.*

Coming back into connection

Generally, we are very disconnected from our bodies and our emotions. Why is that? I think that this goes way back in history, before the Agricultural Revolution. I mentioned in Chapter 2 about how our focus has changed from how the mind of ancient humans worked. If we look again at how people lived at the time, they were hunter-gatherers and spent most of their day outside in nature. They had a powerful awareness and presence in the environment around them and a vast knowledge of animals, plants, rivers, lakes, mountains, valleys, the Earth and the sky. It was very important to be rooted in your senses, your subtle feelings and your intuition. Life depended on it.

As we entered the Agricultural Revolution, we started to own land and grow crops and didn't have the same need to hunt and gather, so spent less time in the wilderness and stayed more or less in one place. With time, more and more people moved away from this way of living, and moved into cities. As I am sure you are aware, the Earth's population has increased dramatically in the last few hundred years, and there is now a lot less space and nature to roam. We also tend to have jobs that keep us indoors or in our car a lot of the time.

Personally, I strongly feel this inner urge to connect with nature on a daily basis and to spend some time outdoors. It simply makes me feel more in balance. So many people have moved away from the connection with nature that they may not even be aware of this need, but it is always present, and you will notice the difference when you do spend time in nature.

So, what has this got to do with your feelings? Well, although we are now living in a completely different society, we are still basically the same as we were thousands of years ago. We have a very basic need to connect with our bodies, with nature and with the environment around us. As there are less and less opportunities to do so, we easily develop disembodiment, i.e. a disconnection with our body, how we feel moment to moment, our intuition and with nature. Often, we are very 'head based' and are trying to 'figure out' our feelings on a mind level. This is when we can get very confused, stressed and anxious, as it is not really possible to find a mind solution to our feelings.

We need to reconnect with our body and allow ourselves to feel the feelings. For example, when we have strong feelings we often don't feel them in the mind, but in the body. Sadness tends to be felt in the throat, chest and belly and we often experience sensations of emptiness, tightness or narrowing. When we experience joy, we tend to feel it in the chest, eyes and front of the body, and there are sensations of expansion, clarity, space and warmth.

Can you be present in the body to the feelings you are experiencing? As mentioned previously, we spend a lot of time and energy running away from our feelings or suppressing them. We are simply scared of strong feelings. However, the more we tend to suppress them the stronger they become, because somehow, they need to be expressed. So, isn't it better to be present to our feelings on a continuous basis rather than bottling them up and then explode later? Or allowing our suppressed emotions to turn into addictions?

Another result of suppressed feelings is that we become ill. The body is desperately trying to tell us that we need to take time to look inwards, be still, present and connect. So always look at the underlying message of anything that goes wrong with your body. What is your body or your True Self trying to tell you? A common example is a cold that doesn't want to go away. It keeps coming back or it doesn't go away completely making you feel bad. What do you think the message behind this is? The message is most likely that you are overriding your need to rest and allow your body to heal and recover properly. Going deeper the message might be that you don't think you deserve to rest and that you need to 'prove' yourself all the time.

When I mentioned this to a client a while ago they said, 'But I *have* to work to earn money and can't afford to take time off.' Why are we so hard on ourselves? Your health and wellbeing are your absolute number-one priority.

Louise Hay wrote in her wonderful book *Heal Your Body: The Mental Causes for Physical Illness and the Metaphysical Way to Overcome Them'* about the connection between thoughts, feelings and illness. She healed herself from cancer by looking at the thought patterns 'beneath' her illness and worked with changing them.

Reflection: Body scan

This exercise should take about 10–15 minutes.

You may want to lie on the floor on a mat. Make sure you are warm and comfortable, by covering yourself with a blanket and resting your head on a cushion or pillow. Alternatively, you can do this exercise sitting upright. Take care to ensure you will not be disturbed for the period of the body scan.

1. Check in with your body just as it is right now, noticing the sensations that are present, feeling the contact the body is making with the floor.

2. Then starting to scan the body, sweeping your awareness through different parts of the body, without judging what you are feeling but as best you can by bringing attention to your experience moment by moment.

3. Starting with the crown of the head, notice any sensations here. It could be tingling, tightness or relaxation or nothing at all. Then move your awareness to your head, feeling the weight against the floor (if you are lying down), then including an awareness of the forehead, and notice how your forehead feels. Then moving onto your eyes, nose, cheeks, mouth, lips, jaw, chin and ears. Being aware moment by moment of the changing pattern of sensations, feelings of warmth, coolness, tightness, ease. If you notice that your mind is wandering, then this is perfectly natural and nothing to worry about. Just gently guide your mind back to the part of the body you are focusing on.

4. Now let go of your head and face, moving your awareness into your neck. Be aware of any tension in the neck and throat.

5. Moving your awareness now to the shoulders, and feel the contact between your shoulders and the floor. Move your awareness into your arms, elbows, wrists, hands and fingers, aware of what is here in each moment.

6. Moving your awareness to your chest area, noticing the subtle rise and fall of your chest with each in and out breath, feeling your ribcage, front and back of your ribs, sides of the ribs, your upper back resting on the floor. Noticing any aches and pains or any discomfort here and seeing if you can bring a sense of gentleness and kindness to these areas.

7. Now bring your awareness to your abdomen and stomach,

the place where we feel our 'gut feelings' and the place of intuition. Be aware of your attitude to this part of your body, see if you can allow it to be as it is. Accepting this part of your body. Then bring your awareness to your lower back, your lumber spine, and then to your pelvis, hip bones, sitting bones, and groin, noticing any sensations or lack of sensations that are here. Develop a loving kindness attitude to this area.

8. Now take your awareness into your thighs and become aware of the weight of your legs, gently noticing any other sensations here. If your mind has wandered off into thinking and day dreaming again then just gently guide it back to this part of the body.

9. Next turn your attention towards your knees, and notice if there is any discomfort here, or there may be no sensation at all.

10. Take your attention into your calves, noticing how your muscles feel here. Notice any sensations in this area. Bring a sense of kindness into your calves.

11. Finally move your attention into your feet, heels, instep, tops of the feet and then toes. Notice whether there is tension here, sensations, numbness, tingling and allowing any tension to soften as you bring a gentle attention to it.

12. Now taking one or two deeper breaths, widen your focus to fill your whole body with awareness, noticing whatever is present, sweeping the body with your awareness from top to bottom, experiencing the body from the inside out. Noticing whether there is any non-acceptance towards any parts of your body, as you fill it with a gentle awareness. Notice if you can have compassion for any judgements or for any tension or pain that might be present as and when you notice it. Feel the life force flowing through you and being aware of this amazing body that you have.

13. Slowly and gently come out of the body scan.

Loneliness

Just as with mental illness, loneliness is something that isn't often talked about. One of the first research studies done on loneliness took place in the late 1970's at UCLA.[1] At the time, the general conception of lonely people was that they were somehow different, and by different, researchers meant uglier, more stupid, less well-educated and stubbornly reclusive. But when the researchers looked at the social status and lifestyle of lonely people they found they were exactly the same as people who didn't feel lonely, i.e. both groups were equally attractive and intelligent, had a similar income and financial status, similar diets and exercise levels, similar education, etc. What they found however was that people who felt lonely seemed tense, restless and inattentive and often had low self-confidence. They also found that people who had a supportive and friendly upbringing were less likely to feel lonely and had more resilience as adults to negative events.

According to the research lonely people have more difficulties opening up and also tend to select relationships badly. They connect with anybody just to avoid loneliness and often stay in bad relationships. What they also discovered was that feelings of loneliness had to do with a person's expectations. If someone feels the need to have one close friend, two friends to go out with, and a partner, and they are missing some of those relationships, they are likely to be lonely. A person with next to no acquaintances who wants to spend a lot of time alone may not feel lonely at all.

Connection

Today more and more people of all ages are feeling lonely. I read somewhere recently that we are now talking about an 'epidemic of loneliness'. We live increasingly isolated lives. Maybe we have moved away from our birth place and our friends and relatives, or maybe we have lost contact with old friends, got divorced or lost our partner. There are many reasons why we could end up feeling lonely.

Nowadays we tend to meet fewer people. We gather less and spend more time on Facebook and other social media sites rather than meeting up. Research also shows that feeling lonely is bad for our health. Prolonged loneliness appears to trigger what is known as the 'fight-or-flight' response, which produces inflammation and so compromises the body's immune system. In other words, loneliness can have a big impact on our health.[1]

If we look back in history, we have a long tradition of living in groups such as family groups, settlements or villages where we were dependent on each other and where cooperation was vital. It is a fundamental human need to connect, with other people, with animals, nature and with something bigger than ourselves. The latest science shows that there is a bond between even the smallest particle of our being, between our body and the environment, between all the people in our lives and in all social groups and societies.[2] All living things succeed and thrive only when they see themselves as part of a greater whole. We have a strong need and urge to connect. Nature has designed us for wholeness and not for competition and domination.

Unfortunately, most of us have grown up in a society that encourages competition rather than collaboration. The whole school system is based on this. Who gets the best grades or are the best at sports? This competitive attitude then continues into our working lives. Who can produce the best sales figures? Who is after your job? In our private lives, it could be about having a better car than the neighbour, being slimmer than your friends, earning more money than your parents, etc. It is about me and mine, and the survival of the fittest. We are living in a strongly ego-centred society and a society that creates loneliness. This is in exact opposition to our fundamental need for partnership, cooperation, balance and living in harmony with our true nature.

We have been taught to think of ourselves as individuals, alone, and in competition with everyone else. This way of thinking is creating separation, within our self and in society in general. The crises that we are facing today are a result of this way of thinking, which is totally at odds with what nature intended. We need to live in harmony with ourselves, other people, our surroundings and the universal force – a vast interconnected galactic superorganism – and we urgently need to re-establish this connection.

We also need to look deep within ourselves and try to understand where the source of these feelings of loneliness come from and look at the patterns all the way back to our early childhood. This includes the environment we grew up in and the feelings associated with this. Did we come from a lonely family environment? Did we miss out on learning how to socialize? Was there a lot of fear, insecurity and stress? What values did you grow up with? Who are you, beneath all the conditioning? Can you allow your heart to speak? We will be talking more about the heart in Chapter 6.

If we look deeper into loneliness, we discover that it often represents a disconnection from our True Self. We may realize that the sadness and frustration we feel is about not being able to live and express ourselves fully. There could be a sense of having lost the connection to the Whole. It is an echo of the disapproval and negativity we may have experienced as children.

I believe that loneliness serves to remind us that we have disconnected from our True Self and from the universal force of creativity. When we feel lonely, it can be a message from the Universe, 'I am giving you the space to listen inwards, and to hear and feel your truth and inspiration'. Feel the feelings of loneliness and cry if you need to. Let the feelings flow. If necessary, find a therapist that can help you with this.

Loneliness vs. solitude

Loneliness and being alone is not the same thing. Solitude can be lovely. Crowded parties can be agony. We need to have time alone. It is in those gaps of 'nothingness' or emptiness that we find ourselves and get to know ourselves better. We will not find ourselves if we cram in lots of activities all day, every day, to keep out the silence and the feelings of loneliness. Instead this will just create more confusion, anxiety, and lack of energy. Embrace times of space and silence and listen to your heart.

I woke up one Monday morning, feeling a bit lonely. I had spent the whole weekend researching and writing this book. Although I love writing, it can be a very solitary experience and I felt that I had spent too much time on my own and in front of the computer. I prayed:

> *Dear Divine, let me experience and be open to connecting*
> *with you and everything around me. Let me experience*
> *friendship and support on all levels. Let me be totally*
> *open to receive.*

The next minute, I looked out into the garden and there were two beautiful goldfinches with red and black heads and yellow on their wings. What a delightful sight! Then one of my students said how much she enjoyed my photos on Facebook. She said, 'When I feel a little low in the morning, your photos cheer me up and make a difference to my day!' I then get an email from another student and he is saying, 'I just wanted to tell you how much I am enjoying your Tuesday evening yoga class, it is helping me immeasurably and I think you are a wonderful teacher' Wow! So basically, be open to receive, connect with the Divine, and see things unfold. It will surprise you!

The shadow

Loneliness can be a part of the so-called 'shadow'. As I mentioned earlier, this term was first used by the psychotherapist Carl G Jung to describe the denied or repressed part of ourselves. We are born whole and were meant to discover our authentic nature (True Self) and every day should be an opportunity to express ourselves and create a meaningful life. There is one thing that robs us of this – our shadow – the dark side, the secrets and our supressed feelings. Our shadow is made up of the thoughts and feelings that we find too painful or embarrassing to accept. So, we repress them and try to hide them. The poet and author Robert Bly describe the shadow as an 'invisible bag that each of us carries around on our back'.

These suppressed feelings or disowned parts may have started with a teacher or parent that called us stupid, the lover who abandoned us or the bully at school. We hide and suppress all the painful feelings we experience. We feel shame and we never talk about it so live in denial. But it is this dark side of ourselves that cuts us off from our True Self. Whatever we have hidden away holds the key to unlock a self to be proud of, a self that inspires us and a self that acts on our dreams.

How do you become aware of your shadow? Start by looking at what you are projecting onto others. When you deny a trait in yourself, you tend to be aware of it in other people. You may react strongly to a quality or behaviour in another, but this is the mirror of that quality in yourself. Also notice the traits in people you admire, as they generally represent qualities of yourself that you have denied. Another way of becoming aware of your shadow is to look at certain repetitive behaviours that you have, for example you may promise yourself, over and over, to eat healthy, stop smoking or drinking but you never do it. Or you may repetitively end up in destructive relationships and do nothing to change this pattern.

I like what Jamie Catto says about shadow work:

> It is about transforming unruly demons into employees
> and harvest the many gifts within instead of exhausting
> yourself battling them.

Here are a few things you can do to identify and integrate your shadow.

1. Look for signs of discomfort, guilt or embarrassment, and also anything that you try to avoid.
2. Realize that there is gold in your shadow, and recast it from being a villain to a teacher. There is so much to learn here and when you transform your shadow you are releasing so much resistance that has stopped you from moving forwards.
3. Call your shadow's bluff. There is a famous story about Milarepa, the Tibetan saint, who came home one night after a long day at work and found his home filled with fire-breathing dragons. At first, he cursed them and ordered them to leave, but they breathed even hotter fire and moved closer to him. He continued cursing them and they continued to advance towards him. Finally, Milarepa stopped, and instead of cursing them, he welcomed them and invited them into his home. Upon hearing this they all disappeared. Call the shadow's bluff like Milarepa did and see what happens.
4. Release your guilt. Guilt is not natural! It is learnt. Is that guilt really helping you? Accept yourself and all your uniqueness.
5. Forgive yourself.

Anger

One of the shadow feelings could be anger and, as the Buddha said, 'Holding on to anger is like grasping a hot coal with the intent of throwing it at someone else; you are the one getting burned.' We hold on to anger because we find it so difficult to handle, so create a façade, a bit like a glossy brochure and we are in the 'approval addiction mode'. In other words, we present a version of ourselves that we hope others will love and accept. This may have very little to do with the True Self. We all walk around with our outer persona, however inside there may be screams of anger, sadness, frustration, stress, hatred, disappointment, etc. Inside of you are feelings and emotions that are not 'OK'.

Anger could possibly be the most misunderstood emotion. It is like a fire inside of you, which is either burning slowly or exploding. If it is misdirected it can cause destruction both in your own life and the lives of others. Most people think that anger is something bad and should not be expressed. That is the message I got as a child anyway. But this is simply not true. Anger needs to be expressed in a constructive way.

While working with clients I have seen how suppressed anger can so often result in physical problems. For example, Jason was overworked and dealt with his anger by playing victim. He would feel sorry for himself for having to work through the weekend. As a result, he developed severe digestive problems. Kim had a difficult relationship with her mother and was angry with her a lot of the time, but wouldn't express it or talk about it. She developed energy problems, and felt tired and lethargic most of the time. These are just a couple of examples how the body tries to 'talk' to us when we don't stay present to our feelings.

When we hold powerful emotions under wraps or deny the expression of these feelings, it is like trying to push a beach ball under water; it just pops back up to the surface again. We can't completely suppress these feelings, so they seep out from time to time, perhaps as a constant low level of irritation or a low or high level of anxiety and worry. And this can result in low self-esteem and low self-confidence and cause you to avoid certain situations. It can also result in major temper outbursts, even to quite minor incidents. For some people anger is an expression of unresolved, long-term deep feelings, such as pain or grief.

When we spend a lot of time harbouring anger, the body reacts as if it's in danger by activating the fight-or-flight response (just as any negative emotions can do), and your body releases the same stress chemicals to prepare your body to respond to imminent danger. When you think of someone who has hurt you deeply, your sympathetic nervous system springs into action in the exact same way, but your body cannot discern the difference, it is an involuntary reaction, releasing the necessary stress chemicals to cope, which get your attention by causing physical changes. We are then in a, more or less, constant fight-or-flight mode, which can have a very damaging effect on the body.

One of the reasons we feel so frustrated is due to not having the opportunity to express our real and True Self. We have compromised and adapted for so long that we have almost forgotten how gorgeous, crazy, creative, fun, colourful and talented we are. We are fed up with living partially and we want to let go of our 'approval addiction'. Often, we have not been allowed to express ourselves fully for a very long time. Sometimes it has been such a long time since we were able to express our uniqueness, that we have forgotten how to. We don't even think there is anything unique about us anymore. I find this so sad and it simply isn't true! We all have a vast number of aspects and qualities that are just waiting to be expressed and come into full bloom. We no longer need to 'edit' ourselves for approval!

Here are a few tips on how to deal with anger:

1. **Think before you speak:** In the heat of the moment, it's easy to say something you will regret later. Take a few moments to collect your thoughts before saying anything – and allow others involved in the situation to do the same.

2. **Express your anger:** Give voice to your frustration in an assertive but non-confrontational way. State your concerns and needs clearly and directly, without hurting others or trying to control them.

3. **Get some exercise:** Physical activity can help reduce stress that can cause you to become angry. If you feel your anger escalating, go for a brisk walk or run, or spend some time doing other enjoyable physical activities.

4. **Take time out:** Give yourself short breaks during times of the day that tend to be stressful. A few moments of quiet time might help you feel better prepared to handle what's ahead without getting irritated or angry.

5. **Identify possible solutions:** Instead of focusing on what made you angry, work on resolving the issue at hand. Is your daughter's room always in a mess? Close the door. Are you stressed, irritated and angry because you have too many things to do? Have a really good look at how you are spending your time and cut out the things that come under the heading 'useless activities'. Remind yourself that anger will not fix anything and might only make it worse.

6. **Don't hold a grudge:** If you can forgive someone who angered you, you might both learn from the situation and strengthen your relationship.

7. **Practise relaxation skills:** When your temper flares, put relaxation skills to work. Practice deep-breathing exercises, imagine a relaxing scene, or repeat a calming word or phrase, such as 'Take it easy.' You might also listen to music, write in a journal or do a few yoga poses – whatever it takes to encourage relaxation.

8. **Know when to seek help:** Know when it is time to seek help from a counsellor or psychotherapist to help you release and deal with your suppressed feelings.

Being an introvert

It took me many years to realize that I was an introvert. I need quite a lot of time on my own to feel good. As a child, I often looked in awe at people who easily made friends and could talk all day (the popular girls in school, for example). How did they do it? I was often lost for words and felt awkward in large gatherings. I was shy and insecure and had difficulties making friends. There were many occasions that were particularly painful at school such as when it was time to choose basketball teams, and I was persistently chosen last (despite the fact that I was one of the best players). I couldn't figure out what was wrong with me and why I was so unpopular. That really did hurt and even when writing this I can feel the pain of rejection that this little girl felt.

What I have learnt with time is that it is OK to be an introvert. Not everyone can be the same, and I have come to accept that I need a lot of silence and time on my own. Of course, I enjoy meeting other people, but for me it needs to be a balance. Too much socializing drains me.

Emotional wounds

Your emotions are incredibly powerful and a great guide towards happiness and inner peace. Your True Self will use feelings and emotions to point you in various directions. The truth is that virtually everyone has emotional wounds. I am sure that all of you reading this have experienced heart ache, disappointment and a whole range of other challenging emotions, maybe relating to relationships, work, family, health, finances, etc.

If you are lucky enough to inhabit an emotionally safe environment, you will start to heal almost immediately after a difficult experience. Others may not heal so quickly and may struggle and be prone to depression, worry, anxiety and addictions. We are moving into a 'tricky' and sensitive area. I am saying this because most of us have huge armour and our emotional wounds are deeply buried. We talked earlier about how we are all presenting a façade or front, when there is so much more going on inside of us. Behind your façade lies the whole depth of the inner you or the True Self, and part of that is your emotional wounds. If we are to live fully, we need to look at all those hidden feelings and emotions.

Take my client Tricia who came to see me complaining about low self-confidence and not being able to pursue her dreams of opening a coffee shop. We talked a lot about the reasons for her not believing in herself and not moving forwards with her plans and dreams. I asked about her childhood, and she said that it was good and that her parents always had been very supportive. However, when we went deeper, it turned out that she was the youngest of seven siblings, and as the family was very poor, she was the last one to receive anything such as clothes, toys and even food. She remembers a painful episode when she was late for dinner, and there was no food left. I knew that we had reached a deeply painful emotional wound, and so did Tricia. By talking about this and expressing the emotions around this, she could finally start to let them go. The next time I spoke to her she had started to make enquiries into renting shop premises.

Reflection: Healing emotional wounds

This exercise can help you to come into awareness of your emotional wounds so that you can begin the healing process.

1. **Remember a difficult experience:** With your eyes closed, recall an emotional experience that is causing discomfort. Try to see the circumstances as clearly as possible in your mind. It could be an experience that revolves around loss or failure. You are recalling an emotional trigger. If you feel that it is a bit too uncomfortable, open your eyes and take a few deep breaths. When you feel less overwhelmed, close your eyes again and proceed.

2. **Feel it in the body:** Notice where in your body you feel this memory. For example, it could be in your stomach or around the heart, or in the throat. Try to locate where you sense it. If you don't feel anything, relax, take a breath, and tune into your body again. You may even feel numb, which is the sign of a deep emotion that has been tied to fear. Everyone eventually feels something in the body doing this exercise. Remember that an emotion is a thought connected to a sensation.

3. **What is the feeling?** Now give your feeling a name. Is it fear or anger, sadness or resentment? Being more specific allows you to focus on the emotional baggage you want to release,

so take the time to tell yourself exactly what you're feeling. To help you, here are the most common painful emotions that people carry around:

- Anger, hostility, rage
- Sadness, grief, sorrow
- Envy, jealousy
- Anxiety, fear, worry, apprehension
- Resentment
- Humiliation
- Rejection
- Shame

4. **Express your experience:** Take some paper and a pen and write down what happened during your painful emotional experience. Put down in detail how you felt, what other people did, and how you reacted afterwards.

5. **Release:** Now take all your pieces of paper and shred them, offering them to the Universe. Feel the release.

Chapter 5

Healing

'Our sorrows and wounds are healed only
when we touch them with compassion.'
Buddha

Your body is a miracle. It will heal itself, given the right conditions. If you cut yourself, the body will heal the cut. If you break a bone, it will heal. It is the same thing with your mind and emotions. Give them a chance, and they will heal. You can heal all those difficult feelings and emotions and experience more peace. Your mind and emotions are self-healing when you don't attempt to deny or suppress your problems and feelings. By getting in touch with them you will start the healing process. Isn't that good to know? Just the thought of that is uplifting and calming.

How do we heal?

When you experience problems or challenges in your life, you may ask: 'How can I change this? How can I create a better life? How can I find more happiness and inner peace?'

My view is that we are already healed. We just don't know it – yet. We have worked so hard at stopping our inner voice from speaking, but our inner wisdom has all the answers. There can be many names for that inner voice, such as the Divine, Universe, God, Buddha, Brahman, etc. It doesn't matter what we call it. I suggest you go with something that feels comfortable to you. I will call it the Divine here. We all have a connection to the Divine or to something immensely powerful and loving. We are here on Earth because of this loving force. We wouldn't be here without it.

The problem is when we disconnect from this force and allow our ego/Conditioned Self to take over. The ego really can confuse us and take us on difficult detours. When we are confused we are not in a situation to make good decisions or to see things clearly.

Of course, we need the ego to function on a day-to-day basis, so the ego is not a bad thing, it is just that most of us have allowed it to take over and run our lives. We seem to have forgotten our deep connection with the Divine or our inner wisdom. We rush from one thing to another and don't take the time to be still and listen to our hearts.

Eckhart Tolle talks about 'the pain-body'. This is a part of ourselves that is locked into or trapped in a 'victim mentality'. The pain-body represents the unaware mind that is a form of unconscious resistance to what is. We, mostly unconsciously, see ourselves as victims. This is a belief that the past is more powerful than the present. We believe that what was said to us and about us in the past is the truth, or what other people did to us is responsible for who we are today. This however is not the truth.

The pain-body is strongly identified with the mind, and so the more you identify with the mind the more you suffer. The more you wake up from your mental ego dramas, the more harmony, joy and balance will fill your life. Feelings such as guilt, self-hate, resentment, depression, jealousy, irritation, etc., are all a form of pain. These feelings either come from the past or are feelings that you create now and that still live on in your mind and body. It can of course also be both.

The pain-body can also be dormant or active. For some people, it is active almost all the time and you might recognize it in those who often complain or are highly critical. For others, the pain-body is only active occasionally when it is triggered by memories of loss, abandonment or abuse.

I often hear the following from clients or friends: 'But *my* life situation is different. *My* problems are bigger and deeper than others, and therefore it is very difficult for me to heal, if not impossible.' However, this is not true. We can *all* heal.

Reflection: Observing your feelings

As soon as you notice that the pain-body starts to become active, it could be in the form of impatience, irritation, feeling low, etc., do the following exercise.

1. Take a few moments to become still.
2. Take a few deep breaths.
3. Just observe your feelings. When you do this, they usually start to subside and eventually disappear. The pain-body can't be active when you are practicing presence.

You might also like to use the following meditation.

Reflection: Metta or loving-kindness meditation

The original name of this practice is metta bhavana, metta meaning 'love' (in a non-romantic sense), friendliness, or kindness; bhavana meaning 'cultivating': 'loving-kindness' for short.

1. Take a few moments to become still. Become aware of yourself and focus on feelings of peace, calm, and tranquillity. Then let this awareness grow into feelings of strength and confidence, and then develop into love within your heart. You might like to imagine golden light flooding your body, or a phrase such as 'May I be well and happy', which you can repeat to yourself. These are ways of stimulating the feeling of metta or love for yourself.

2. In the second stage think of a good friend. Bring them to mind as vividly as you can, and think of their good qualities. Feel your connection with your friend, and your liking for them, and encourage these to grow by repeating 'May they be well; may they be happy' quietly to yourself.

3. Then think of someone you do not particularly like or dislike. Your feelings are 'neutral'. This may be someone you do not know well but see around. You reflect on their humanity, and include them in your feelings of love.

4. Then think of someone you actually dislike – an 'enemy'. Try not to get caught up in any feelings of hatred for them but think of them positively and send your metta to them as well.

5. In the final stage, think of all four people together – yourself, the friend, the neutral person, and the enemy. Then extend your feelings further – to everyone around you, to everyone in your neighbourhood; in your town, your country, and so on throughout the world. Have a sense of waves of loving-kindness spreading from your heart to everyone, to all beings everywhere. Then gradually relax out of meditation, and bring the practice to an end.

All we need is love

It is amazing what a difference a meditation like this can make. John Lennon wrote, 'All we need is love' and this is so true. All we need is to love ourselves. By doing that we can find more peace within and that means loving yourself exactly as you are now, and in exactly the circumstances you find yourself right at this moment.

Anita Moorjani writes about this in her book *What if This is Heaven?* In 2006, she was extremely ill with terminal cancer, and had a powerful near-death experience (NDE) in which she experienced a love and acceptance beyond words. She writes: 'Being in that state made me realize that I didn't have to do anything to deserve being loved. I realized that I am loved unconditionally just because I exist.' She says in many places in her books that it was this love that healed her.

So, why not take a moment and try to imagine this vast, unconditional love and see how you are bathing in it at all times? It is there for you always.

Saying yes (after having said no for a long time)

When I was in my 20's I met a very charismatic and rather eccentric man 14 years older than me. He had travelled the world and I was *very* impressed. He was so much fun, and we instantly fell in love and married shortly afterwards. We travelled Europe together in a VW campervan and had some fantastic times. I loved the adventure, all the fun and interesting people we met and would not have liked to miss this for the world. I learned how to let go of some of my insecurities and to say yes to adventure. In that sense, he was a great inspiration and I am very grateful for that.

However, as time went by and we settled in London I started to discover another side to him. A dark, destructive and intensely jealous side. What had started as a light-hearted and fun adventure turned into struggle, fear and negativity. He loved me in his own way but could not let me be myself. I felt incredibly suppressed, lonely and fearful. My life started to become very limited, as I was only 'allowed' to do certain things and meet certain people. He made sure I didn't visit my home country for over three years. I was heartbroken.

The effect of this was that I started to say 'No' to my heart and soul and to my True Self, and I became someone who had to please him and behave in a certain way to keep the peace at home. I am sure that many women, and men, can recognize this scenario.

As I started to sink deeper into despair, I found it very hard to see any light ahead. Life was challenging and I just tried to survive as best as I could. I couldn't believe that I had ended up in such a difficult situation. Then one day my husband's best friend turned up at my house. I had no idea what he wanted but he started to explain that he could no longer just watch me being bullied and suppressed by my husband. He said, 'You have so many talents and such a bright and beautiful future ahead of you. You *have* to leave your husband.'

I was totally stunned and didn't know what to say. Somehow, I didn't think that anyone had noticed how bad things were. But, of course, he was right. We had a long chat and I can't thank him enough for caring so much. A few days later I plucked up the courage and said to my husband that our marriage was over. He was shocked but agreed that it had come to an end. We parted as friends and have remained friends ever since. I would like to add that I have no bad feelings at all for my ex-husband. I have totally forgiven him and moved on.

I am telling you this story because it was such a big turning point in my life. I had denied my True Self for so many years, even before this marriage. I had said 'No' to my True Self so many times, and it was time to take my power back and move from victimhood to empowerment. I won't pretend it was easy. There followed a time when I struggled a lot, as I mentioned right at the beginning of the book.

Another important turning point came when a friend suggested that I read Louise Hay's book *You Can Heal Your Life*. I went out and bought the book and read it in one day. I could not put it down! It came exactly at the right time and was exactly what I needed. In her book, Louise says that we are 100 per cent responsible for our life. A strong 'yes' emerged from deep within myself. I knew that this was very, very true. I had feelings of euphoria and I could literally *feel* how my strength was coming back into my life. It was not up to other people, the economy, society or anything else how my life turned out. It was up to me.

This was when I finally started to say 'Yes' to myself and to my heart. A huge YES! It was the beginning of a wonderful healing journey.

So how can we come from a No to a Yes? Are you ready for the biggest YES of your life?

The YES flow

What tends to happen when you start saying 'Yes' is that your energy increases. I mentioned above that I felt euphoric when I started acknowledging my own power and I have noticed this with my clients as well. When we are in denial about our true nature, we lack energy and motivation, and find all sorts of excuses for not moving forwards. When we start taking steps in the right direction, we suddenly have all the energy in the world. For example, I had a client who was transformed when she quit her job as a university lecturer. She had suffered for years in a difficult and suppressive work environment. When she left her job, it was as if a big, heavy weight had lifted of her shoulders, and her whole energy changed. She smiled and looked so much more relaxed. She was open and chatty while before she was very quiet. She had a wonderful new energy.

You may experience energy surges in smaller ways. For example, you may be patiently listening to a friend's list of health problems, and then she mentions a fun holiday that you had together years ago, and you suddenly feel a lift in your energy. Or you may be visiting your in-laws listening to their complaints about how wrong everything is in the world (feeling very tired suddenly), but then decide to stay up all night watching your favourite TV show.

What kinds of activities increase your energy levels? Do certain people make your energy increase? What places makes you feel uplifted and energetic? Can you recall times when you felt a surge of energy?

> ### Reflection: The YES energy
>
> - In your journal make a note of three things that make your energy surge (for example: a chat with your best friend, a walk on the beach, reading an inspirational book, meditation, planning a holiday).
>
> Did you notice that your energy increased just by thinking about these things?

Your health

Science has shown how our health and energy are directly affected by our thoughts and feelings. Dr Candace Pert, a ground-breaking neuroscientist, helped to create the foundation for an entirely new interdisciplinary branch of science called 'Psychoneuroimmunology' (PNI). Dr Pert's research provides scientific evidence that a biochemical basis for awareness and consciousness exists, that the mind and body are indeed one and that our emotions and feelings are the bridge that links the two. She explains:

> The chemicals that are running our body and our brain
> are the same chemicals that are involved in emotion. And
> that says to me that we'd better pay more attention to
> emotions with respect to health.

This new science explains how we are one system; the brain is integrated into the body at a molecular level and therefore neither can be treated separately without the other being directly affected. According to Dr Pert, our bodies are in fact our subconscious minds. We discussed Embodiment in Chapter 4 which ties into this.

So, in other words, what you think and what you feel moment to moment has a direct effect on your body and all its functions. If you repeatedly think negative thoughts, it lowers your immune system, and makes you more susceptible to disease – anything from a cold or headache to (maybe eventually) cancer and other more serious diseases. On the other hand, if you repeatedly think positive and uplifting thoughts, you will have a more robust immune system, which will protect you from ill health.

Like so many others, sadly I also have known many people who have been diagnosed with cancer, and have often noted how they have been dealing with feelings of sadness, fear, disappointment for perhaps 20–30 years or more before the cancer 'turned up'.

Sometimes you may not even be aware that you have a fair amount of negative thoughts and feelings, until you drop them. I have met many people who are desperately hanging on to difficult situations – a marriage, a job, etc., and when they finally quit the job or end the marriage, their health improves dramatically.

As I was writing this book, I twisted my knee doing gardening and had very limited movements for a while. However, I made great progress and the knee started to feel more like normal again, and then I injured it again! This made me look at healing in a deeper way. I did everything I could on a physical level such as eating a super healthy diet, taking the right supplements and doing the right exercises. So, I now had to ask myself what was going on at a deeper level. What were the deeper reasons I was experiencing this issue? I believe that everything that manifests on a physical plane is a result of what is going on at a metaphysical level. After some reflection and meditation, I realized that I had been particularly stressed and under pressure the weeks before the injury and I was disappointed with myself for scheduling so many things when I needed to rest. I also received some bad news regarding a close relative. I was stubbornly hanging on to my busyness and not adjusting to my needs of rest and relaxation (knee problems often represent inflexibility). I also had a flashback to when I was about eight or nine years old and had severe knee pain and was unable to go to school.

Reflection: YES to health

Try to remember three times in your life when your health seemed better than usual. What was going on in your life at that time?
Make a note of them in your journal.

Reflection: Time disappeared

When you do something that you really enjoy, have you noticed that time 'disappears'? For example, when you were little, you may have been out playing and suddenly your mum called that it was time for dinner? You felt like you had played for 10 minutes when in fact several hours had gone by.

- Write down the types of activities that make you forget what time it is.

Chapter 6

The Heart

'If the 20th century has been the Century of the Brain... then the 21st century should be the Century of the Heart.'

Gary E. R. Schwartz, Ph.D.,
and Linda G. S. Russek, Ph.D.,
authors of The Living Energy Universe

There has been some very interesting and exciting research into the heart in the last few years. For a long time, science believed that the master organ in the body was the brain. However new research has found what they call 'the little brain' situated in the heart.[3] This is extremely significant and may forever change how you think about yourself and your life. This is the key to creating a balanced life, to find inner peace and to move in a direction you want. It can help you to tune into your purpose and passion. It has certainly had a major impact on many aspects of my own life and how and what I study and teach.

Often, when one of my coaching clients is confused about an issue or has difficulties making a decision I ask them, 'What would your heart say?' They often find that their heart responds with love and wisdom while their mind responds with fear, opinions and negative beliefs. They find that the heart represents their True Self, intuition and intelligence while the mind tends to represent (often) negative messages that we picked up in our childhood.

This is no coincidence. As mentioned above the latest research shows that the heart contains a little brain in its own right. The human heart, in addition to its other functions, actually possesses a heart-brain composed of about 40,000 neurons that can sense, feel, learn and remember. The heart brain sends messages to the head brain about how the body feels and many other things.

The conversation between the heart and the brain

Until the 1990s, scientists assumed that it was only the brain that sent information and gave commands to the heart, but now we know that it works both ways. The heart and the brain are constantly communicating with each other. The heart's nervous system, 'the heart brain', is a complex network of several types of neurons, neurotransmitters, proteins and support cells, like those found in the brain in the head. The heart communicates, via the nervous and hormonal systems, as well as other pathways with the brain and acts independently of the cranial brain. Amazing!

Scientists at The Heart Math Institute in California have found that the heart, like the brain, generates a powerful electromagnetic field. What is even more astonishing is that they found that the heart generates the largest electromagnetic field in the body. Previously they thought the brain generated the largest electromagnetic field. The bio-electrical field as measured in an electrocardiogram (ECG) is about 60 times greater in amplitude than the brain waves recorded in an electroencephalogram (EEG). The magnetic component is approximately 5000 times stronger than the brain's magnetic field and can be detected 5–8ft (1.5–2.5m) away from the body with sensitive magnetometers. When I first read this, I had to stop for a minute to just take it in. Wow! But wait, there is more!

Bruce Lipton, an American developmental biologist and author of Biology of *Belief* (best known for promoting the idea that genes and DNA can be manipulated by a person's beliefs), says:

> The electromagnetic field generated by the heart is the most powerful rhythmic electromagnetic field produced by the body. The heart's field permeates every cell and may act as a synchronizing signal for all the cells in the body in a manner analogous to information carried by radio waves.

What exactly does this mean? We now know that the heart and the brain are constantly communicating with each other. The good news is that we can intentionally direct our heart to communicate with our brain and body in beneficial ways.

For example, when we experience sincere positive emotions, such as caring, love or appreciation, the heart processes these emotions, and the heart's rhythm becomes more coherent and harmonious. This information is then sent to the brain and to the entire body – neurologically, biochemically, biophysically and energetically. You can shift into this coherent state to bring your mind and heart into harmonious alignment. By doing this you will develop better access to your intuition. When we have better access to our intuition – and when our brain and heart are in a coherent rhythm – the body, including the brain, begins to experience many different benefits such as greater mental clarity, better intuitive abilities and better decision-making.

Also, we now know that when we are focusing on thoughts and feelings of gratitude, forgiveness, compassion, joy and love we are creating electromagnetic waves in the heart that influence not just our mind and body but, even more astonishing, what is going on around us and the events that are taking place in our life. We are influencing the energy field around us. At the same time, we are communicating with the Universal field (as mentioned in Chapter 1). Gregg Braden, scientist, author and visionary, talks about how we are constantly, via our thoughts and emotions, communicating with what he calls 'The Blueprint in the Higher Dimension'.

We often think that we are on our own and that what happens in our lives only has to do with us, but according to ancient wisdom and the very latest research, this is not true. We are in constant communication with our body, mind, everyone around us and the whole Universe. In fact, we are part of a huge Universal energy field. One example is that when you feel happy and contented everyone around you will pick up on this. Your heart is communicating the feeling of happiness with everyone else's heart in your surroundings.

The implications of this are astonishing, because it puts the power back into our own hands (or hearts!). As you learn how to merge the senses of your heart and the logic of your brain into a single potent system, you empower yourself to beneficially manage change in your life.

Heart-based living

We now have a new understanding of the heart as a dynamic, connecting, creative intelligence. We are starting to learn how to connect the physical, emotional, intuitive and spiritual aspects of the heart. This changes how we think, act and relate and is called heart-based living.

As we tune into our heart, we raise our vibration and create a more inspired and fulfilling life. As more and more of us start living in this way, we influence everything and everyone around us, and thereby raise the energy of the whole planet. Yes, we are living in exceptionally stressful times, but at the same time more and more of us are developing self-awareness and an awareness of our thoughts, feelings, behaviour and energy. With this awareness, we can empower ourselves and others. And as Nick Williams says in his book *The Work We Were Born to Do*:

> *One aroused and awakened heart can touch and feed*
> *millions of people with love and nourishment.*

The global situation that we are experiencing right now is partly a result of emotional turbulence, from collective emotions in responses to terrorism, wars, floods and other instabilities. It is a wave of stress that is stirred up and made bigger by media. At the same time the media and Internet help us to connect and work towards a better world. There are countless action groups being formed that are working towards improvements in healthcare, ecology, equality, etc., which in turn creates more acceptance and connection between people and can also be very empowering and inspirational.

If I ask you to point to your real self, most of you would point at the heart. When you live from this level you are moving away from stress, competition and striving and into the intuitive knowing of the heart. We have become used to living our lives from the mind, but now it is time to live from our heart instead.

How to become more heart-based

There are many ways that you can become more heart-based and create inner and outer harmony. The idea is to synchronize your heart and brain waves, so that they work together. This is called 'coherence' and it creates harmony on all levels of your being.

Lack of coherence between the brain and the heart affects your ability to listen, your mental clarity, feeling states and level of sensitivity. When the brain and the heart are in coherence it is the opposite, you are efficient, have a clear mind, listen attentively to others, make better decisions and are feeling good. This is of huge importance.

There are many simple techniques that can teach us how to listen to, and follow, the intuitive information of the heart. We can learn how to make better decisions, feel more balanced and to use the power of the heart to manage the mind and emotions.

Here is an exercise that I have found very useful.

Reflection: Creating balance

This is a quick technique for when you are feeling stressed, out of balance or would like to feel more in harmony. This is much more than positive thinking; it creates a clear, heartfelt shift in how we view a situation, an individual or ourselves.

1. Whatever you are doing, stop for a moment and take some time out.
2. Take your attention away from the overactive mind or any disturbed emotions and into the area around your heart. You might like to visualize that you are breathing through your heart to help focus your energy in this area. Keep your focus here for a few seconds.
3. Recall a positive, fun feeling or experience and attempt to re-experience it right now.
4. Using your intuition, ask your heart, 'What would be a better response to the situation, one that will minimize future stress or imbalance?'

5. Listen to what your heart says in answer.

This an effective way to get your reactive mind and emotions in check and find a better solution! You may hear nothing, but perhaps feel a little calmer. You may receive verification of something you already know, or you may experience a complete shift and be able to see things in a more balanced way. Although we don't always have control over our experiences, we do have control over our perception of them.

Making good decisions

I am sure that you have been in one or more situations when you just didn't know what to do or what decision to make. Maybe it was a question about what to do about a specific health problem; maybe it was about leaving or staying in a relationship, a long-term investment, or an important business or career decision. We can become terribly stressed about 'getting it right', churning over the options in our mind, again and again. We are trying to solve the problem with the logical mind alone, forgetting about the heart.

We encounter many different challenges throughout our life and most of them are best solved with the heart and mind together. If we try to solve a problem or find an answer to a big question with the mind alone, our decisions are often overshadowed by past conditioning, old beliefs, past experiences and negative thinking. If, however, we focus on the heart, and work on creating a heart-brain coherence, the decision can come to us quickly. Your heart already knows the answer, before you have even asked the question! Your heart has true knowing and wisdom and knows instantly what is true for us in this moment.

When we learn how to combine the senses of the heart with the logic of the brain, we create a potent system of empowerment and can handle the changes in our lives in a much better way.

Reflection: Heart-based decisions

I often use the following technique for decision-making, which was inspired by an exercise from Heartmath.[4] It can be anything from small to big decisions. Remember that your heart's intelligence is always with you. You can trust it.

1. **Focus on your heart:** Allow your awareness to move from your mind to the area of your heart. In this way, you turn inwards and move away from the outside world.

2. **Slow down your breathing:** Take a few slightly slower breaths than usual, counting to four on the inhalation and four on the exhalation (approximately four seconds on the inhalation and four on the exhalation). Do three or four rounds. This is stimulating the parasympathetic branch (relaxation response) of the nervous system and helps you to relax. Have a sense that you are letting go.

3. **Generate positive feelings:** Start to generate genuine feelings of care, appreciation or gratitude for anything or anyone. It is the quality of your feelings that are important here. Sincere and heartfelt feelings. You are now starting to improve the coherence between your heart and your brain. Everyone can experience this, but it may sometimes take a little training. To generate positive and loving feelings I often think about the dog I used to have and how much I loved him. Or I might be thinking of a wonderful holiday I had.

4. **Ask your heart a question:** You can ask anything you like, small or big. I recently used this question to ask if I should book a venue in Italy for one of my yoga retreats. And in the past, I have used it to choose anything from a financial advisor to a hairdresser. I have used it for asking about the timing of many of my events. It can be questions about a decision you have to make about your health, relationship or home, or anything else.

5. **See what comes up:** Notice any feelings in your body. Or any spontaneous thoughts or images that come up. Write it down in your journal. If nothing comes up immediately, notice if you get an answer later.

The yogic heart

I think it is interesting to see how the importance of the heart was known thousands of years ago. In Yoga philosophy, the heart and the heart centre (heart chakra) are at the centre of the seven chakras (energy system) and have a central role in all human beings. In the spiritual traditions of India, the 'heart' refers not so much to the physical organ as to a psycho-spiritual structure corresponding to the heart muscle in the body. This spiritual heart is celebrated by yogis and mystics as the seat of the Supreme Self and is called *hridaya* or *hrit-padma* ('heart lotus').

According to Ramana Maharshi, the great Advaita Master:

The godly atom of the Self is to be found in the right

*chamber of the heart, about one finger-width's distance
from the body's midline. Here lies the Heart, the dynamic
Spiritual Heart. It is called hridaya, is located on the right
side of the chest, and is clearly visible to the inner eye of
an adept on the Spiritual Path. Through meditation you
can learn to find the Self in the cave of this Heart.*

In yoga philosophy, when we talk about 'withdrawal of the senses' (pratyahara) which is one of the eight limbs of yoga, we centre ourselves in the chest area, looking for the deepest aspects of our being, and we start to connect with the heart. In this way, we move from the busy mind to a receptive, contemplative disposition. It is a kind of surrender, which implies lucidity and discernment. We are moving into a space of peace and sacredness.

Intuition, which comes from the heart, is said to be Divine, because it represents a direct participation in the universal spiritual wisdom. The heart, which is also called the 'Spiritual Sun', is considered to be a place of revelation, the vital centre of being, and the source of the deepest intuition. It is a sacred symbol. The Spiritual Master Mooji says:

*All the mind-streams eventually flow into the One ocean
of Beingness. There are many pathways for the mind;
there are no paths for the Heart, for the Heart is infinite
and fills everything.*

Yogic philosophy states that we have seven major chakras or energy centres in the body. Each centre represents one aspect of our being. Without going into the details of each chakra here, one way of seeing the chakras is that the three lower chakras are the creative chakras and the three higher are related to thought and logic. The middle chakra or fourth chakra is the heart chakra or heart centre.

Simply put we can say that our emotions are based in the three lower chakras (1st–3rd chakras) and our thinking is based in the three higher chakras 5th–7th chakras).

7th chakra – crown – *Sahasrara*
6th chakra – third eye – *Ajna*
5th chakra – throat – *Vishuddha*
4th chakra – heart – *Anahata*
3rd chakra – solar plexus – *Manipura*
2nd chakra – sacral – *Svadhisthana*
1st chakra – root – *Muladhara*

Let's say that you have always dreamt of becoming a singer. You think about this in your three higher chakras (thoughts), but for this to manifest, or become reality, you need to include the three lower chakras (emotion and creativity). These two energies then meet in the middle, i.e. in your heart chakra. The magnetic field of the heart centre then changes and starts to communicate this energy into the world around you. The heart is communicating 'I am a singer'. When you *feel* this in your heart, you start to make this a reality. You start to manifest it.

Thought + Emotion = Feeling/Energy/Manifestation

There are only two emotions – love or fear. It is interesting to see that the three lower chakras also represent the early part of our life. The first Chakra (1–8 years old) represents standing up for oneself. The second Chakra (8–14 years old) represents challenging social conditioning. The third chakra (14–21 years old) is about developing self-esteem/self-confidence. Take a moment to think about the kind of environment you grew up in. Was it based on fear or love? The lower chakras also represent our subconscious and often we are not aware of what we are 'carrying' with us on this level.

So, the emotions (love or fear) + our thoughts create feelings. Those feelings are an indication of what you are likely to experience in your life. For example, fear-based feelings might be anger, sadness, disappointment, fear, irritation, jealousy, guilt, anxiety, grief, sorrow, doubt, worry, distrust, despair, frustration, etc. Love-based feelings might be optimism, gratefulness, peacefulness, inspiration, assertiveness, confidence, elation, joy, decisiveness, serenity, trust, etc.

It is not possible to have love-based feelings all the time. We need to acknowledge that there is a whole spectrum of feelings including all the 'negative' feelings we may have as discussed earlier in Chapter 4. We need to accept what is going on in the moment but make sure that we are not getting stuck in negativity permanently or for very long periods of time. We talked about the 'pain-body' earlier which basically is a place of negativity/stress/depression that has become our identity. This is largely mind based and we need to be aware of that, and instead connect more with our heart.

Reflection: Manifesting from your heart

Often, you know what is not working in your life or what you don't like, but what about what you *would* like? What would you like in your life? If for example you would like a new job, imagine how you would you FEEL when you have this job? Focus on the feeling. This is the key.

1. Take a moment to get still. Close your eyes. Take a few deep breaths. Relax.
2. Allow your awareness to drop from the head to the heart. Focus on your heart.
3. Focus on feeling love, warmth and appreciation for your life.
4. Now think about a quality that you would dearly like to have

in your life (it could be love, inner peace, creativity, fun, health, freedom, excitement, stability, etc.).

5. Visualize how it would be to have this quality in your life.
6. Feel the feeing in your Heart. Really focus on the feeling. Amplify it. Breathe slowly and deeply. Relax.
7. Come out of the mediation. How did it feel? Write down any thoughts, feelings, impressions, messages, etc.

Filling up your container with love

Being heart-based also means loving yourself. When I start speaking about this in my workshops, I often feel the atmosphere changing and the audience becoming tense! Why? Because this is a sensitive subject for many people, as so many have difficulties in this area. Nobody told us that it was OK to love ourselves. Instead you may have been criticized during your childhood or just generally experienced a lack of support. As soon as we pick up these negative messages about ourselves, it strongly affects our self-confidence and self-belief as a grown up.

A common response from clients is, 'But surely we can't just love ourselves, we have to love other people first. It is selfish to love ourselves.' Most of us spend our time trying to love others, but we never seem to take time to love ourselves. This creates imbalance and unhappiness. We are trying to get love from others, but our own 'love container' is empty. So how can we give love from an empty container? It doesn't work.

So, imagine now your 'love container' and imagine that everyone else on the planet also has one of these love containers. These containers can't tip over. So, in order to spill our love into another person's container, our container has to be full. How would you fill up your 'love container'?

When we have enough, we are naturally drawn towards sharing. This then becomes a joy. We feel abundant. It is time to fill up your own 'love container'.

Reflection: Filling up your love container

Make a list of ways that you could show love to yourself.

1. Ask yourself: 'What are some ways that I can think of to show love to myself?'
2. Note down all the ways you can think of. The more the better.
3. You can also ask yourself: 'What would someone who loves themselves do right now?'

Examples:

- Writing a list of positive aspects of myself.
- Letting go of fear and taking more initiatives.
- Trusting my heart.
- Allowing myself more time to enjoy life.
- Stop living life by other people's values and beliefs.
- Treating my body with respect.
- Asking for help when I need it.
- Applying for the course I have always wanted to do.
- Making time for meditation.
- Saving more money for my dream holiday.
- Keeping a journal.
- Not comparing myself to others.

When you have written down all the ways that you could love yourself more, how does it feel?

Chapter 7
Awakening

'I am other than name, form and action.
My nature is ever free!
I am Self, the supreme unconditioned Brahman.
I am pure Awareness, always non-dual.'
Adi Shankara, Upadesasahasri 11.7

We often seek happiness outside ourselves. And we're so used to living in this way that we find it difficult to 'hear' what our heart is telling us. It is as if we are living in a self-made prison and think that life is *supposed* to be that way. However, everyone can wake up from this and experience freedom. When you are waking up from being over-identified with your thoughts, you feel fully alive and present in the now. This feeling is similar to being in the zone, being in love or sharing quality time with a good friend. This is the foundation of living life fully.

When we are awake, we often have a strong sense of wellbeing and feel love and peace within ourselves. In this state, we no longer identify with our worried and stressed thoughts or our fearful feelings. They have to a large extent lost their power over us and we have shifted out of our chattering mind. We are experiencing the freedom that was already there. We have peeled away the layers of conditioning. This happened to me when I started meditating, and we'll explore more of the benefits of meditation in Chapter 9.

You and I are the same

As we discussed earlier, we think that we are separate from everyone else, and that we have to handle everything on our own. We struggle, fret and go on 'mind trips' in an attempt to figure out what to do and how to live – all on our own. Our minds get *very* busy, *very* full and *very* confused. I used to be like this, and I still have bouts of 'mental dramas', but nowadays I recognize these almost instantly. I sometimes laugh out loud when I discover what my mind is doing, and realize that it is OK, and that I can let it go. Of course, sometimes it isn't so easy to let go, but just the awareness of what is going on in your mind can help.

Advaita Vedanta, one of the classic Indian paths to spiritual realization refers to the nonduality of your true nature; Advaita literally meaning 'not two' or nondual. This Oneness is a fundamental quality of everything. Everything is a part of and made of one nondual consciousness. People, animals, plants and objects are different in appearance, but they are all connected at their source – they come from the same source. Advaita says that this one Being is behind all life and has an infinite number of different expressions, and you are one of them. The loneliness we explored in Chapter 4, for example, is an inability to fully understand and connect with this.

What does Oneness mean?

When we attempt to look at something in isolation, we often find that it is in some way part of something much bigger. For example, a single wave is not separate from the sea. A flower is not separate from the plant. Your foot or hand is not separate from your body and so on.

We find it difficult to understand what Oneness is because we are so used to seeing things as separate. Of course, each of us is a unique individual, and this uniqueness isn't removed by being part of one unified whole – far from it. Our purpose *is* to be individual and unique, and to find our own path. At the same time, we are a part of a larger whole and everything we see around us is part of this Oneness. Everything, that's humans, animals, plants, the earth, the sun, the Universe and beyond, are all made of intelligent energy.

Reflection: Oneness

Imagine that you are the whole Universe; you live in total joy and bliss. Imagine that there is no past or future, only now. Imagine there is no space or time, just eternity. Imagine endless peace, harmony, and unconditional love. Imagine that there is no fear. This is Oneness.

Experiencing Oneness

So, can we *truly* experience Oneness? Yes, but only by direct experience, moving beyond the mind, intellect, and ego. Oneness is always with us as the underlying essence of everything. However, we have to go beyond the senses and beyond duality to find Oneness. We have all had glimpses of Oneness, maybe when you saw your newborn child for the first time, or when you saw a particularly beautiful scene. We may have said, 'It took my breath away' or 'Time stood still.' This is Oneness. We became at one with the totality of the experience. When we return from the moment of Oneness, we find it impossible to express it. It just was! There are no words to describe Oneness.

In *Vedanta* it's simply referred to as *Tat*, which means that.[5]

We can also have a direct experience of Oneness through meditation, which is a systematic path by which our awareness settles to a quieter level of thinking. All duality is in the realm of thoughts. When we slip into the spaces between our thoughts, we are in a state of Oneness. Oneness isn't an experience, it is a state of being.

Quantum physics describes a unified field, which underlies and connects everything in creation. Who we are, is pure consciousness or Oneness, expressing itself in different forms at different times in our evolution.

We have largely forgotten that we are all One. As a result of forgetting, we create an illusory world of duality, which often leads to suffering. All arguments, conflict and wars are due to the belief that we are separate. When we realize we are One, who, or what is there to fight against? On a cosmic level, two people fighting is as ridiculous as if your hands decided they didn't like each other and started a fight.

Here are a few suggestions of how you can experience more Oneness.

- **Community**: Being part of a supportive community helps us to experience Oneness. Community helps us on our own journey and allows us the opportunity to help others. It helps us open to new and different ideas and to begin to dissolve our resistance and limiting beliefs. Community can connect us to a sense of Oneness.
- **Meditation**: This simple practice can give us a direct experience of Oneness deep within ourselves. When we let go of the over-active mind, we enter a field of pure awareness. This opens the door to higher states of consciousness and the full re-integration of Oneness in our lives.
- **Being conscious:** Begin to become more conscious of everything in your life. Be conscious of your thoughts, emotions, and how you react to situations and people in your life. Try to be conscious of your choices.
- **See your own Oneness**: When you stand in front of a mirror, pause for a moment, and look directly into your eyes. Say silently or aloud 'I am the Universe' or 'I am Oneness'. This is your soul reflecting into itself and reminding itself of its Oneness. Practice this as often as you can.
- **See the Oneness in everything**: The *Bhagavad Gita* states, 'If you can see God (the Oneness) in everyone, you can never do harm to anyone. Wherever you go, whatever you experience through your senses, keep reminding yourself that it is all part of the same Oneness. Begin to recognize the world as a

reflection of yourself.

- **Namaste**: The Indian blessing *Namaste* (pronounced 'nam-ass-tay') is accompanied by bringing the palms together in front of your heart centre, when meeting or saying goodbye to someone. It means, 'I recognize the Divinity in you which is also the Divinity in me' or in other words, 'We are the same Oneness.' If it's not comfortable for you to say it aloud, think it silently every time you meet someone.

- **OM**: Oneness is the potential for all sounds but is, itself, silent. In every moment of existence, the whole of creation is constantly emerging from the silence of Oneness. The first sound or vibration emerging from the silence is OM. This vibration then expands into all the sounds and vibrations of the Universe. When we chant OM it draws our awareness back to the dawn of creation, and into Oneness.

Being heart-based

Love is the greatest, most powerful unifying force in creation. In the *Vedanta* it says,

> The ignorant person (engrossed in duality) desires
> material things; the intelligent person (seeker on the
> path) desires enlightenment; but the wise (knower of
> Oneness) just loves and receives everything.

Live your life from love and recognize that you are the Universe. Be the Oneness.

Chapter 8

Inspiration

'Often, we don't know how thirsty we are until we have a
drink and, similarly, we often don't know how much we need
inspiration until we experience it.'
**Nick Williams,
Author of 'How to be Inspired'**

I often ask my clients: 'What inspires you? What is your passion?' But often
they reply, 'Hmm, what inspires me?... hmm... What am I passionate about?
No, I have no idea.'

Generally, we don't talk that much about inspiration. After all, isn't that
something artists' experience? Did anyone ask you as a child what inspired
you? When you were in your teens and it was time to choose an education
or a career, were you encouraged to choose something that was 'secure'
and 'stable' rather than what was fun, interesting and made your heart sing?
Perhaps, it is not surprising then that so many of us find it difficult to answer
this question.

I remember one client, who after much thought said, that her chi gong
teacher inspired her greatly. 'So why can't you be like that?' I said. I could see
the surprise on her face. It had never occurred to her that she could be like her
teacher. Of course, inspiration is not about copying someone else, but I could
sense that there was a lot of insecurity in the way my client expressed herself.
It was almost like inspiration and aiming high was for other people, not her.
It doesn't have to be like this. Everyone can feel inspired! It is our birth right.

Defining inspiration

Here are some things that we came up with during one of my YES weekends
when we were brainstorming what inspiration can mean:
- Excited
- Passionate
- Doing what you love
- Have a vision
- Heart-based
- Following my intuition
- Listening to my intuition

- Listening inwards
- Soul based
- Profound wellbeing
- Magic
- Feeling light and happy
- Creative flow
- Original and innovative
- Feeling exhilarated
- Feeling alive
- Motivated
- Joyful and exited
- Feeling connected with the Divine
- Warm heart

Reflection: What inspires you?

So, I ask you now: What inspires you?

You may have at least part of the answer to what inspires you in the Reflection: 'Time Disappeared' in Chapter 5.

If you feel a little stuck, the following hints might help get you started:

- Who inspires you?
- What uplifts you?
- What makes your heart sing?
- What are you passionate about?
- What do you love doing?
- When do you feel at your very best?
- What are you good at?
- What are your talents?
- What films, music, books, creative pursuit, teachers/ speakers inspire you?
- Who are your role models?
- What makes you happy to be alive?
- Who makes you feel good about yourself?

You can also do the following exercise to give you an idea of what inspires you.

Reflection: Bookstore

Go to a bookstore or library. Look through the shelves and see what attracts you. Which books are you drawn to? Which books make you curious? Let it be fun and playful. Pick five or six books. Sit down and have a look at them. Is there a specific message in the books for you? How does it feel?

Inspiration

Inspiration is not just something that happens occasionally but should be a part of your day, every day. The word 'inspiration' means 'breathing in', and we are all breathing in (and out) every day. In yoga, the breath is at the centre of all practices, such as yoga postures, some meditations and specific breathing exercises (*pranayama*). It is the link between body and mind, and has a balancing effect on our whole being. According to yoga philosophy we are taking in *prana*' (meaning energy or life force) via the breath. There is no life without the breath. Alexander Filmer-Lorch writes in his wonderful book *'Inside Meditation'*: *"Our life starts with an inhalation and ends with an exhalation, and there is great significance in this fact. Our breath is invisible like the wind yet it makes us part of something mysterious and undiscovered, which we call the 'Unknown' that forms an intrinsic part of infinity."*
Are you breathing deeply and fully, or are you holding or restricting your breath? A restricted breath is often associated with fear.

Inspire sounds similar to *spirit*. This is especially appropriate because when we're filled with prana or life force, we often feel inspiration. Inspiration can also mean love, joy and peace. We need to connect daily to this energy to feel good. If we are constantly putting inspiration last on our list of 'things to do' we are not treating ourselves very well. Make sure that you have some time each day to do something inspirational, such as going for a walk in nature, reading something inspirational, meditating, etc.

Inspiration needs to flow 'through' you, just as the breath does. And it needs to fill you. Imagine breathing in a beautiful light, which fills your body. On the in-breath it enters your body, inspiring you, and on the out-breath it flows out of you, inspiring others! If you connect with inspiration, you will also inspire others.

Reflection: Breathing in inspiration

Take five deep full breaths right now. Inhale fully and completely and exhale fully and completely. Visualize that you are breathing in Inspiration and let it fill you. And visualise that you are letting go of any fears and restrictions on the outbreath. Let the inspiration flow out to others on the outbreath! Enjoy the feeling.

Yogic breathing

As mentioned earlier breathing is a central part of yoga. In this context, I am referring to Hatha Yoga, the physical branch of yoga most familiar in the West. One of the reasons we feel so good when we practise yoga is that we take deep, even breaths that oxygenate every cell of the body. Deep breathing also balances the nervous system, taking us out of the fight-or-flight mode and brings us back to a calm state.

Pranayama is the fourth of Patanjali's eight limbs of yoga and it means 'to extend the life force'. Research has shown how mindful breathing, i.e. paying attention to your breath and learning how to breathe in the most effective ways helps to lower everyday stress levels and improve a variety of health factors ranging from mood to metabolism.[6] Pranayama is a physical health practice, mental health practice, and meditation. It is not just breath training but also mind training and can improve our wellbeing on all levels.

Even though our breathing is an automatic function, most people have a lot to learn and improve when it comes to the most basic of our physiological functions. The number of breaths per minute should be around 12, but many people tend to take between 14–22 breaths per minute, which is too fast. People who practise yoga regularly often take 5–8 breaths per minute, and their breathing is generally much more efficient.

Breath and inspiration are linked to each other as mentioned earlier, so by improving your breathing you also create a foundation for being inspired – every day!

Reflection: Breathing (Pranayama)

This Pranayama exercise is called Samavritti Pranayama, which means equal inhalation and exhalation. Sama means same, even or equal (i.e. the inhalation and the exhalation is equal in length), vritti refers to the fluctuations of the mind. This exercise is soothing and calming and can help to balance the mind.

1. Take a moment to centre yourself.
2. Close your eyes.
3. Take a couple of deep breaths. Relax.
4. Breathe in for 4 counts (4 seconds). Breathe out for 4 counts (4 seconds).
5. Do 10 rounds.

Resistance

Sometimes when we feel that we want to follow our inspiration and make changes in our lives we encounter resistance. As I mentioned earlier, it is far too easy to stay in the same old dysfunctional situation rather than change it. This is when we see fear rearing its ugly head. The True Self desperately wants change, but your ego/Conditioned Self comes up with all sorts of excuses for not changing – everything from worrying what others will think to questioning our own abilities.

Nick Williams says in his book *Resisting the Soul:* 'Resistance is largely unconscious.' We often don't even know that we are in resistance, but we are experiencing it in the form of boredom, irritation, anger and restlessness. On a deep level, we know that we need to change. Ask yourself why you are bored/irritated/angry/restless. What is wrong? What is not working right now in your life? Where do you need change? Try to learn from these feelings. Allow the resistance to lead you in the direction of your inspiration.

Signs that you are in resistance:
- Procrastination – 'Oh, I will do that tomorrow.'
- Self-sabotage – you allow opportunities to just slip away.
- Supporting other people's success instead of your own – so there is no time left to focus on yourself.
- Just seeing obstacles – 'It won't work anyway. I am too old. I don't have the money.'
- Excuses – 'I don't have the time. I must wait until the kids have grown up. I am not talented enough.'
- Not the right time – 'I have to wait until...'
- Lack of self-belief – deep inside you just don't believe that you can do it.
- Big dreams and no action – you are good at visualizing and dreaming, but fail to take action.
- Concerned with what other people think – others will think I'm crazy or won't support me.

Will you allow resistance or your inner critic to rule your life, or will you go with inspiration and what your True Self wants? Take it step by step. You don't have to make massive changes all at once. Look at what baby steps you can take today, to take you in the right direction. For example, I don't recommend that people just quit their job and then hope for the best but start making some changes.

One of my clients, Sharon, worked at a large financial company. She was unhappy in her job. She wanted to work with personal development. We discussed what steps she could take. The first thing she did was to sign up for a life coaching course and then started to see a few clients. At the same time, she cut down on her work hours at the financial company. After a year Sharon had built up a good client base, and she was also teaching personal development workshops and was writing a book. Eventually she was able to resign from her job and is now a published author. Sharon didn't just suddenly quit her job, but took things step by step, so that she felt that she was in control and so that she felt that the change was at a comfortable pace for her. As you can imagine Sharon is now a very different person from when she worked full time in a job she didn't like.

Did you know that you were created to be innovative, creative and with the ability to change how you perceive your reality? You have the freedom to choose to look at the world with excitement and curiosity and to honour your infinite ability to learn, create and grow. Right now, in this moment you can choose to see the world from a new viewpoint. You can choose to expand your vision and move beyond your perceived limitations and bring into your life things that may currently only live in your thoughts, desires and imagination. It is in your power to do this.

Chapter 9
Meditation

'When you can quiet the fluctuations of your mind and drift
into stillness & silence, you can finally hear the whispers of
your heart... the whispers of god.'
Davidji

Meditation has been a part of my life for over 20 years. To be honest I would find it very strange *not* to meditate. When I first started meditating, I had periods of a steady practice, and then periods of no meditation at all. But as time went by I really began to notice the difference when I didn't. Every time I meditated I felt calm, balanced and usually felt good for the rest of the day too. Through regular practice, I developed more patience, both with myself and other people. I also noticed that I could handle challenges much better. It was as if I was developing an inner stability or resilience. I wasn't so easily rocked by events, people or circumstances.

I also found that meditation works on many different levels. Not only did I feel an inner stability, but I also got more in touch with my emotions such as anger, fear, joy and compassion. Emotions would come and go, and I was able to feel them, watch them and then let go of them. This was profoundly healing.

Many times, we don't want to look at our emotions, but in meditation we are in a calm and balanced place, and that makes it much easier to get in touch with what is going on inside. So instead of suppressing our emotions we can allow them to come and go and thereby process them in a balanced way.

The spiritual teacher Swami Chidanand Saraswati says, 'Meditation gives you direction. It is your inner GPS.' I totally agree.

Meditation and stress

When I first started to teach yoga and meditation in the 1990's, I was surprised at how prevalent stress and stress-related problems were. Now, many years later, it is even worse! Many people come to a crucial point when they feel that they simply must do something about their stress levels. Instead of relying on medication or stimulants, they now increasingly turn to meditation.

However, people meditate for all sorts of reasons, not only to deal with stress, but also to improve relationships, understand themselves better, tap into their potential, increase creativity, find meaning and purpose in life and awaken their spirituality. Whatever your reason is for trying meditation, it is an effective way to experience a sense of peace and wellbeing.

In the past, many people thought that meditation was something strange or only practised by monks on mountain tops. I am pleased to say that this perception has changed radically. One reason for this is that there is now overwhelming scientific research showing the many incredible benefits of meditation. Numerous studies have indicated the many physiological benefits of meditation. For example, an eight-week study conducted by Harvard researchers at Massachusetts General Hospital (MGH) determined that meditation literally rebuilds the brains grey matter in just eight weeks. It's the very first study to document that meditation produces changes over time in the brain's grey matter. The study involved taking magnetic resonance images (MRI) of the brains of 16 study participants two weeks prior to participating in the study. MRI images of the participants were also taken after the study was completed.[7]

'The analysis of MRI images, which focused on areas where meditation-associated differences were seen in earlier studies, found increased grey-matter density in the hippocampus, known to be important for learning and memory, and in structures associated with self-awareness, compassion and introspection'

One of the major benefits of meditation is that it takes you out of the fight-or-flight mode. You may remember how we talked about how the fight-or-flight response served us in ancient times by helping us to survive in a dangerous environment. However, it is important not to become stuck in fight-or-flight mode as it is so damaging for our health and wellbeing. Meditation stimulates the opposite branch of the nervous system – the parasympathetic branch – the relaxation response.

Can anyone meditate?

Many people don't think they have the temperament for meditation, have tried it briefly only to give up, or they see it as an esoteric discipline without application to their lives. But with practise, anybody can meditate. The problem is that meditation is often confused with relaxation or some other special state that we have to get to or feel. Some people try to meditate and don't feel that they are getting anywhere or feel anything special, so they think that they are one of those people who can't do it. However, meditation is not about feeling a certain way or experiencing anything in particular. It is about being still and feeling the way you feel. It's not about emptying the mind and getting rid of all thoughts, although with time you will experience more stillness and fewer thoughts. The meditation teacher and author Davidji says:

> Our thoughts are not roadblocks to our meditation, they
> are the divine expression of the universe and the building
> blocks of infinite possibilities available to us in every
> moment.

Above all, meditation is about letting the mind be as it is and relaxing into that. It is not about reaching a certain goal, but about allowing yourself to be in the moment. It is really very simple, but we love to make it complicated!

Look and feel younger with meditation

Did you know that regular meditation can make you look and feel 10–20 years younger, increase health and longevity, and prevent brain-deterioration, dramatically changing what we previously thought were inevitable processes?

Recent research reveals that meditation lowers the stress chemical in the blood called 'cortisol'.[8] Excess cortisol kills brain cells and leads to cognitive decline. Meditation also increases the blood flow to the brain, which results in less memory loss. It also lowers blood pressure and other markers of ageing and enhances psychological well-being. One of the most important discoveries is that meditation preserves the length of the telomeres (end cap of our DNA) which is a very important marker of ageing and longevity: longer telomeres equals less illness and longer life.

The slow brainwaves produced by meditation also promote the release of healing, growing and rejuvenating hormones such as DHEA (dehydroepiandrosterone), melatonin and serotonin. DHEA is a hormone that helps the body fight viral, bacterial and parasitic infections, prevents inflammation and supports the thymus gland (which programmes cell lifespan).

During deep meditation, activity slows dramatically in the areas of the brain responsible for the release of stress-related substances such as cortisol and adrenaline. This whole-body/mind deep relaxation promotes healing, cell repair and cell growth. The relaxation that comes about through meditation is far deeper even than sleep. Although DHEA does decrease naturally in the body during the course of a lifetime, there is no reason not to boost DHEA levels through the practice of meditation. Other benefits include:

- Relief from stress and anxiety (decreases the production of stress hormones)
- Takes you out of the fight-or-flight mode
- Lessens fear, loneliness and depression
- Enhances self-esteem and self-acceptance
- Improves concentration and clarity of mind

- Resilience against pain and adversity
- Increases optimism, relaxation and awareness
- Helps prevent emotional eating, smoking and other unhealthy lifestyle habits
- Improves your mood and emotional intelligence
- Increases mental focus
- Increases memory retention
- Better cognitive skills and creative thinking
- Better information processing
- Improves the health of the immune system
- Improves energy levels
- Improves breathing and heart rate.
- Decreases blood pressure and hypertension.
- Lowers cholesterol levels
- Lessens inflammation
- More efficient oxygen usage
- Increased production of the anti-ageing hormone DHEA
- Improves sleep
- Deeper understanding of our true Self
- Higher degree of connection with Oneness

Reflection: How to meditate

A common misconception about meditation is that you have to sit a certain way, but all you have to do is place yourself in a position that is most comfortable to you. It could be sitting cross legged or sitting on a chair, it is your choice.

Try the following simple meditation practice daily, start with 5 minutes and then slowly build up until you're meditating for 15 minutes each day.

1. Sit in a comfortable seated position with your spine straight.
2. Take a few deep breaths, and relax.
3. Allow your breath to settle into its natural rhythm.
4. Count your breaths, as inhalation – 1, exhalation – 1, inhalation – 2, exhalation – 2, and so on up to 10 and then start again on 1. Do two to three rounds.

Reflection: Tibetan Buddhist 9 breath purification

If you found the previous exercise too tricky, try this simplified Tibetan Buddhist breathing exercise before your meditation. You can also do this breathing exercise on its own.

1. Come into a comfortable, seated meditation position.
2. Bring your hand up to your nose and use your right thumb to gently close off your right nostril. Breathe in and out three times through your left nostril.
3. Now use your ring finger and gently close off your left nostril. Breathe in and out three times through your right nostril.
4. Lower your hand and breathe in and out three times through both nostrils.

Making time and space for meditation

The most common reason I hear for not meditating is 'I don't have time'. However, anyone can find 10–15 minutes each day for meditation. This is a long-term investment in you, your health and sanity. If we don't allow ourselves time for silence and stillness, we may be heading for trouble physically, emotionally, mentally and spiritually. So, think of meditation as part of your self-care routine, as you would washing your face or brushing your teeth.

Find a peaceful space in your home where you can spend time in meditation, maybe create a 'sacred space', a place where you can recharge, renew, and find more peace and inspiration. You might place a particular object here, such as a statue, picture or candle that has meaning to you.

Choose a time to meditate that works for you. It doesn't necessarily have to be in the morning, but could be when you get home from work, last thing at night or any other time that fits in with your daily routine. Make this a habit and explain to other members of the family that this is your meditation time and that you must not be disturbed. Stick with this!

Other rewards of meditation

I find that teaching meditation is extremely rewarding, and I have heard some wonderful accounts of how meditation has changed people's lives. One of the most common responses is that people didn't realize just how stressed and out of balance they were before starting meditation and how they notice a huge difference after just a few sessions. As I mentioned previously, in my experience meditation helps to develop a basic calm 'foundation', which helps enormously in daily life. Here follow a couple of responses from participants:

The meditation course was the kindest thing that I have ever done for myself. I practise nearly every day. I used meditation to recover from a major operation, and it

*helped me cope with pain and speeded up my recovery.
I now feel the healthiest I have felt in years. I feel I have
a much better quality of life and my relationships with
close family and friends have greatly improved, I'm more
understanding and aware of other people's needs and
feelings. I also feel I understand my body on a deeper
level and have learned to listen to my body and its needs.
Overall I have a much more positive attitude to life.*
Natalie

*I practise meditation every morning, and I'm also trying to
practice mindfulness when I'm walking, both of which I'm
finding have made a difference in my life. My life is busy
(I live with my family, three generations in total), always
involved in the crazy world of children and grandchildren.
Since I have developed a regular meditation practice,
I have a real sense of inner calm and am less inclined
to get caught up in all the busyness. This year I made a
conscious effort to stop doing some things I wasn't really
enjoying and to create space from people who seemed to
drain my energy. This would have been difficult for me to
do in the past, as I've always found it hard to say 'No'. Not
now! I'm much clearer in my thinking, more decisive and
overall, much more at ease with myself and my beliefs.*
Wendy

Reflection: Beginner's body scan meditation

This is a great beginner's meditation where you become more aware of
your body and any tension you are holding in different parts of the body.
You will notice how you start to release the tension as you do the practice.
This meditation only takes a few minutes and can be done anytime during
the day when you feel tense or stressed or just want to find your calm.
You will find a longer 'body scan' meditation in Chapter 4.

1. You can do it sitting upright in a chair or lying down. Once
   you are comfortable, close your eyes, take a few deep breaths
   and then let your breathing find its own natural rhythm.
2. Starting from the top, focus on each part of the body in turn
   while saying to yourself:
3. I am relaxing my face.
4. I am relaxing my neck.

5. I am relaxing my shoulders.
6. I am relaxing my arms and hands
7. I am relaxing my back.
8. I am relaxing my chest and abdomen.
9. I am relaxing my hips and buttocks.
10. I am relaxing my legs and feet.
11. Start again from the top.
12. Repeat the body scan a few times until you feel calmer.

Deeper aspects of meditation

We now have an understanding of how meditation affects the body and mind, but meditation can also take you to places you never thought possible. Most people are first drawn to meditation as a way of handling stress, but the dimensions of meditation are many. To me it is the central pillar of my life. This may sound dramatic, but I remember my meditation teacher often saying, 'You organize your life around meditation, not the other way around.' I now understand what he meant. Meditation is so important that it has to come first. It is a priority. I find that how I react and perceive things in my life is a direct result of my meditation practice. If I don't practice meditation my inner balance may not be so good but if I stick with my meditation practice I come from a much more balanced place.

Mindfulness

Are meditation and mindfulness the same thing? Yes and no. These days whenever 'meditation' is mentioned, people tend to think of 'mindfulness'. It's one of those amazingly successful names. It's both a quality – the quality of being aware or paying close attention – but it has also become a sort of 'brand name'.

When it comes to meditation, mindfulness is a very specific practice. It is a derivative of the Buddhist practice known as *vipassana*. It has become well known through the good work of teachers like Jon Kabat Zinn and others who took the vipassana practice and did scientific studies about its effect on the brain, mood, health and wellbeing. The same things that made it a good test subject are the same things that make it such a well-known method of meditation: it is very simple. It is just sitting and paying attention to what arises in the body and mind. There is no mantra, no talk of spirituality, no guru, or anything except for a simple, gentle focus on what is happening. With such comprehensive scientific research behind it, it has been adopted by the modern Western mainstream society as *the* meditation method. However, this is just one of many, many meditation practices.

Let's look at this in the yogic context. Mindfulness comes from Buddhism, and Buddhism is a derivative of yoga, the mystical, practical practice that comes from India. In yoga, we never take one technique or one teaching as a one-size-fits-all solution to anything. The Sanskrit word for practice (one of them) is *upaya*, meaning 'remedy' or 'means'. You can think of a practice as a remedy or something we do to create inner and outer balance. So, the many yogic practices such as physical asana (yoga postures), mantras, meditations, breathing exercises, acts of service, etc. are seen as an array of tools to help us in different ways. Meditation, in the yoga tradition, is a toolbox within the toolbox. It is not one practice, but a whole category of yoga practice.

Let's say we're just talking about sitting meditation (there are so many others including movement, walking, lying down meditation, and so on), there are literally hundreds and hundreds of meditations. Mindfulness – sitting and quietly paying attention to whatever arises – is one type of meditation practice and so is its mother practice, *samatha vipassana* – sitting and quietly observing the movement of one's breath. A meditator might repeat a mantra (silently our out loud), or watch their breath, or combine a mantra with their breath, or visualize chakras – energy centres, or focus on the heart. There are so many options.

The yoga approach to meditation is to learn a variety of skills to be capable of finding inner balance. However, it is important to spend time with one meditation technique at a time and learn it fully before trying another. But over time, it is good to learn a variety of different meditations so that we can really help ourselves and take ownership of our practice. The problem with assuming that meditation means mindfulness practice is that, for many people, sitting silently clearing the mind and watching the breath can be difficult and even a bit boring. So, they give up. Meditation is like a large and beautiful garden with many different flowers and plants. It's a toolbox full of sophisticated energetic techniques and tools to unlock our hearts and minds and for people who have a spiritual intention, it's a practice that brings us into direct conscious contact with the Divine within our own hearts.

Chapter 10
Miracles and Manifestation

'Miracles occur naturally as expressions of love.'
A Course in Miracles

Do you believe in miracles? I do!

According to Wikipedia a miracle is 'an extraordinary and welcome event that is not explicable by natural or scientific laws and is therefore attributed to a divine agency.'

I was at my desk one morning preparing for a coaching/astrology client when a message appeared in my email inbox. It was from one of the venues I use for my YES weekends. They were very sorry, but they'd had to cancel my booking for one of my weekends, as someone wanted to hire the whole venue on that same weekend (I hire half the venue as I work with smaller groups) and would give them preference. I was disappointed, but quickly closed my eyes and prayed: 'Dear Divine, please allow me to teach and spread my message of inspiration at this weekend. I trust in you.' I kept it short as my client was just about to arrive.

After my client had left I went back to my office to check my emails. There was a message from the venue again. 'Sincere apologies for any inconvenience that we may have caused you. We deeply appreciate you as a client and would like to let you know that your weekend booking is secure.'

A miracle? Yes, I think so and I was hugely grateful. If the Universe wants you to move in a certain direction, you will be guided.

Synchronicity

Deepak Chopra says that synchronicity is 'choreographed by a great, pervasive intelligence that lies at the heart of nature, and is manifest in each of us through intuitive knowledge.' And as I have been writing this book, I have had the most remarkable 'coincidences'. Almost all the material in this book has been handed to me from one source or another. I may have the impulse to take out a book from the bookcase that I haven't looked at for a very long time, and on the first page I turn to, see the answer to something I have been thinking about. I have received emails with the exact material that I needed at a certain point. I've discovered workshops that I was meant to attend, to further my own development and that have been very useful for this book.

I've found newspaper articles containing valuable information and had whole passages of text coming to me at night in my dreams.

Carl Jung, the psychoanalyst who popularized the word synchronicity, believed that these kinds of coincidences hinted at his patients' destinies, orienting them in the right direction for self-actualization. He also thought that synchronicities might show up just to confirm that a patient was on the right track. Once, a patient of Jung's had a vivid dream about a scarab, a large rare type of beetle. In a session with Jung, the client was trying to figure out what the scarab represented and there was suddenly something tapping at the window of Jung's office. Jung opened the window, and there sat the beetle, waving its antennae at the patient!

The term synchronicity means 'things happening at the same time' and is sometimes used to mean a coincidence so remarkable it seems beyond chance. I have experienced many small and big 'coincidences' or synchronicities. Here are a few.

Once when I was getting ready to go to a yoga teacher training workshop, I looked in my wardrobe and wished I had a black t-shirt to go with my leggings. I then hear the post arriving, and there was a small parcel on the floor. Can you guess what was in the parcel? A black t-shirt! Out of the blue Nike had sent out black t-shirts to its yoga customers!

Here is another one.

Years ago, when I split up from my husband and my finances were in a very bad state, I was really, really struggling. It was New Year's Eve, and I only had a couple of pounds in my pocket. That was all the money I had. In the morning, I had said my prayers for financial help and visualized a positive outcome. I decided to go into town and go to a café and have a cup of tea. It was cold and snow was falling on the ground as I walked through town. Suddenly I saw something glimmering in the snow. It was a pound coin! I looked around to see if anyone had dropped it from their purse, but there was nobody around. I bent down to pick up the coin, only to discover that there was another one hiding in the snow, and another one, and another one... In fact, there were so many pound coins that they would not fit into my purse! Suddenly a man turns up to help me pick up all the coins. I tried to explain that it wasn't my money, but he just didn't listen and just handed me the coins. I looked around again to see if there was somebody who had dropped the money, but there was nobody. I just couldn't believe my luck and I treated myself to a cup of tea and a large piece of cake!

Around the same time, I was desperate to find a job. Every day I would spend a lot of time in prayer and visualizing finding a good job. I would also write down what I wanted. I focused on this with all my heart. I went in to town one day and, as I walked passed a recruitment agency, there was a very big sign filling up the whole window space saying, 'Swedish speaking PA wanted for local company.' As you know I am Swedish, but I live in semi-rural Kent, so the chances of this type of job coming up in my area was miniscule. I stopped and just stared at the sign. I couldn't believe it. I wasn't even dressed presentably, standing there in jeans and trainers, but I just went straight in and said, 'Hello I have seen the position in the window and I am Swedish!' I got the job and this saved me financially, and I was able to keep my lovely house.

My clients, especially after one of my YES weekends, have reported similar synchronicities. After having spent much of the weekend focusing on what it is they want in life (and letting go of all the limited thinking), little miracles happen. For example:

- Linda had divorced her husband almost two years previously and was living in rented accommodation. She had been looking for a house to buy for ages but just couldn't find anything she liked. She was also hoping to meet a new partner. On the Monday after the weekend, she was viewing a house and instantly fell in love with it, made an offer there and then on her dream home. She also signed up for an online dating agency (something she previously really didn't want to do) and had her first date that week. She met a lovely man and they are still together!
- Christina was doing admin work for various companies and had been at the same company for six months. Her contract was about to end. She loved her job and wanted to stay, so she focused on keeping the job. On the Tuesday after our weekend she was offered a one-year contract and a pay rise!
- Anna was 62 and had just been made redundant. She felt a bit lost and said that she didn't want to retire just yet. She focused on what she wanted, and the next week she landed a great job at a drama school!
- John had his flat on the market and was hoping to sell it and move to a bigger place. He sold it the day after the YES weekend.

When we take time to focus on what we really want in life, we open up to exactly that. We open up to inspiration and we open up to miracles. Anything is possible. Yes, I mean that, absolutely anything can come true but if we keep spending time with our inner critic or allowing resistance to rule, we limit what I call the 'Yes flow' or 'Divine flow'.

Think about it like this. The Divine *wants* to express itself through you. It is waiting for you to *allow* it to flow through you. When you open up, and stop resisting, it can start to flow. This is when you get in touch with your uniqueness, your brilliance, your inspiration, your True Self. So, ask yourself,

'What wants to be expressed through me?'

Living on purpose

When you are doing what you were meant to do, living on purpose, you benefit the world in a wonderful and unique way. Remember when we talked about the energy field earlier. When you do what you love, you radiate love, joy and inspiration. Your energy field brightens, your life brightens and everybody else will also benefit from this. You will experience true love, inner peace, abundance and many other things.

You might be saying, 'But I don't know what I want. I don't know what to do with my life or which direction to go. In fact, I am really scared.' That is actually a great starting point. You are at the threshold of change. You know what you *don't* want, i.e. all the things you noted down previously in Chapter 2 when you explored five things you would like to change. Now it is time to focus on what you *do* want.

Reflection: Three things you want

- Write down three things that you would *love* to have in your life or would *love* to be. Think big! The important thing here is to connect to your heart. We have already talked about the significance of the heart and how being heart-based changes everything. Allow your three things to really come from the heart. What makes your heart sing? What truly inspires you?

Example:

Nick: I would love to have more success with my band, find really good, creative and fun musicians to work with, and go global with our music. I also dream about having a house by the sea where my wife and I can live.

Now it is your turn, note down the three things that you really want.

If you have a trusted friend or partner, tell them how you would **FEEL** if you had this in your life. Really go for it and describe it in as much detail as you want. If you don't have a friend or partner available, write it down in your journal.

You have now worked up some juice! Doesn't it feel great to focus on what you *do* want and what is important for you? Unfortunately, for most people this is rare, but it really shouldn't be! Talking about, focusing on and feeling what is important for you is crucial for your happiness, and as you have learnt from my stories above, once you really do focus on what you want, it often happens quickly.

Manifesting

As I mentioned previously our thoughts, feelings and beliefs eventually manifest in our lives. So, for example if you persistently have negative thoughts and feelings about yourself you are much less likely to move ahead in the direction of your dreams and desires. Your negative thoughts and feelings are manifested as low self-confidence, lack of self-worth, a passive attitude, a victim mentality, etc. On the contrary if you have predominantly positive thoughts and feelings about yourself and your life, you are much more likely to manifest positive situations, relationships, circumstances and events. What you think and feel manifests.

This gives you huge power. You are free to manifest what you want in life. It is a bit like driving a car. You are the driver holding the steering wheel and deciding where you are driving. You have a goal in mind and you are making your way there. There are lots of other cars on the road, traffic lights, pedestrians and many other things. If you let go of the wheel there will be chaos and possibly also accidents. Your car will probably smash into other cars or come off the road. So, you can decide to hold onto the wheel and avoid those situations. This is how your life is. You either have the power to decide your direction, or you let other people and circumstances take over. This is the difference between empowerment and disempowerment.

Reflection: Light beam manifestation

Look at what you wrote down in the previous exercise – three things that you want. Then do the following meditation.

1. Close your eyes. Take a few deep breaths. Relax completely.
2. Visualize or imagine a large beam of light in front of you, coming from above.
3. Place your wish (what you want) in the middle of the beam.
4. Let it sit there for a while and absorb the light. It is being infused with spiritual energy. Focus on it. Make it vivid. Feel the power of this.
5. Bring your wish into your heart and let it sit there for a while, now being infused with heart energy.
6. Know that this is coming true and that you are co-creating with the Universe.
7. Come out of the meditation.
8. Write down any thoughts or feelings in your journal.

Just after I had written the above I was looking at my diary and it happened to fall open on 20 April 2012. That day I had written down my wish and it went like this: 'I am in the future and I am on holiday in Flåm in Norway. It is such a beautiful place and the journey there is amazing. I absolutely love it here. We stay in a lovely hotel and I am so grateful for this.' I had been looking at holidays in Norway for some time and found information about Flåm and it looked so beautiful, and I knew I wanted to go there. Three years later I received a birthday present from my partner and you guessed it, it was a holiday in Norway, including Flåm! We had such a lovely time visiting Oslo, Flåm and Bergen and it was one of the best holidays of my life. Never think that what you are focusing on will not come true!

Focusing on what it is you want does not mean that you should not be living in the now. We have already talked a lot about how important it is to live in the present moment and being present to what is. You will notice that by focusing on what it is you want to manifest in your life, you create a lot of good feelings *in the present moment*. You are focusing on what you want, from your heart, and with that you are creating good vibrations in your own life – in the present moment. You will feel good. People may comment on how bright and positive you seem.

Reflection: Inspired action

As you work with what it is you want, your goals, dreams or intentions, both your conscious and subconscious mind will be focused strongly on *what it is you want*. You have established a connection with your inspiration and with your heart.

- Listen to any thoughts, ideas and feelings that may come up as you do this work, and follow the ones that feel strong (say 'Yes!'). This will lead you to take *inspired action*. Write them down in your journal.

Example:

Many years ago, as I worked with the goal of running yoga retreats abroad, I suddenly came up with the idea of contacting some Spas abroad to ask them if it would be possible to run a retreat there. I took inspired action. This led me to contact a spa on the west coast of Sweden and I will now have my 12th retreat there! (and if you are interested in this retreat and other retreats have a look at my website www.innerlightyoga.co.uk).

Flow

Once you start tuning in to what you really want in your life, spend time focusing on it and take some action, synchronizations will take place, as we talked about earlier. It is as if the Universe can't wait to show you the way and to co-create with you. You are in the yes flow!

When you are in the yes flow, you allow inspiration to come through you. You listen to your intuition and follow it. Once and for all you leave behind all those negative beliefs, self-criticism and anything else that is sabotaging your dreams and goals. When this happens, you are expressing your True Self.

Ping – a message in my inbox. It is a friend's request from someone called Barbara Berger (from Goodreads). Most of you probably have no idea who Barbara Berger is, but I have been a huge fan of her writings for many years and she has truly inspired me and been a big influence on my work. So, to get a friend's request from her was astonishing and I accepted immediately. I took a look at her page and then her website, and discovered that she had written a new book. I ordered it. At the same time, I took one of her previous books out of my bookcase. I had not been looking at it for some time and immediately got some new ideas and inspiration. Was this a coincidence? I don't think so. The Universe gave me some inspiration to move along with writing this book.

Affirmations

I am sure that many of you have heard of positive affirmations. This is when you replace a negative thought with a positive one. Louise Hay is the expert on this and first described how to use them in *You Can Heal Your Life,* which has sold 50 million copies worldwide. When I first read this book in 1991 it changed my life. I had such a strong and powerful awakening while reading it. It made perfect sense to me. I realized that I had given away my power for far, far too long. Louise explained that you can have a wonderful life, but you have to focus on what you want and not on what you don't want.

I have used affirmations for many years. It is important however that your affirmations come from your *heart*. Often, we repeat affirmations but have not dealt with the underlying beliefs, and then wonder why we don't get any results. Affirmations can't just be mind-based but need to go much deeper in order to be effective. There needs to be a strong *feeling* connected with the affirmation, so that we can invite it into our world. This is not just a practice that we do a few minutes a day, but we need to *live* this way, so that our whole life becomes a big and powerful heart-based affirmation. We are saying 'Yes' to life from the heart!

Reflection: How to work with affirmations

Affirmations can also be called 'intentions', and they can help to reprogramme your subconscious mind and eliminate negative beliefs, as well as replace fears and doubts with confidence and certainty – and so take you into a higher vibration of happiness, appreciation and gratitude. Here is how you work with them.

- Start with the words 'I am'. These are two very powerful words representing your True Self.
- Always use the present tense.
- Affirm what you do want, not what you don't want.
- Keep it brief and specific.
- Include a dynamic, positive feeling word.
- Make the affirmation for yourself, not for others.

Here are a few examples:

- I am so grateful that I have completed my degree and found a wonderful job.
- I am so happy to live in my new home by the sea.
- I am celebrating how healthy I am and how well I am feeling.
- I am feeling calm and focused in all situations at work and at home.
- I am enjoying quality time with my children every day.
- I am delighted that I now have a successful, fun and interesting job/business.

Here are a few words that you can include and that are self-affirming and uplifting:

Alive, amazing, blissful, brilliant, bold, calm, cheerful, clear, confident, creative, decisive, delightful, divine, dynamic, excited, fabulous, focused, free, fun, glorious, grateful, inspired, joyful, light, magical, magnificent, miraculous, optimistic, passionate, positive, powerful, proud, radiant, receptive, relaxed, proud, satisfied, spectacular, strong, terrific, unlimited, vibrant, whole.

Now it is your turn. Write down in your journal one or more positive affirmations, that come from your heart.

Chapter 11

Gratitude and Forgiveness

'When you arise in the morning, give thanks for the morning light, for your life and strength. Give thanks for your food and the joy of living. If you see no reason for giving thanks, the fault lies with yourself.'
Tecumseh (1768–1813),
Shawnee Native American leader

A powerful way of saying *yes to life* is to practise gratitude. In the previous chapter, we focused on what we want, how to take inspired action and how to work with affirmations. Working with gratitude is like working with a potent affirmation; a way of focusing on what is good and positive and attracting exactly that into your life.

The power of gratitude goes back a very long way and is a central part in many religions. Buddha said that you have no cause for anything but gratitude and joy. Krishna said that whatever he is offered he accepts with joy, and Jesus said thank you before he performed a miracle. Looking at many of the indigenous traditions from the Australian Aborigines to the American Navajo and Cherokee, to Tahitians and Eskimos, gratitude is at the centre of their practice. There are also many, many people that made gratitude a central part of their lives, such as Mother Theresa, Gandhi, the Dalai Lama, Leonardo Da Vinci, Plato, Shakespeare, Proust, Descartes, Jung, Newton, Einstein just to name a few.

All those people knew the importance of practising gratitude and yet today its power has been largely forgotten. Instead we often complain, and forget how lucky we are and how much we have to be grateful for. Gratitude brings us out of victimhood and into our hearts, and it is from here that we can change our energy and experiences. Gratitude can turn relationships around, improve our health and happiness, improve our circumstances, job and many other things. Best of all, it is free and available to anyone.

Do you remember when you were a child and got excited about Christmas or the summer holidays? Or maybe you got excited about your new bike or doll. Life was magic! We want to get back to that sense of magic, fun, excitement – and one way of doing that is to practise gratitude. Practising gratitude is saying yes to life.

There is an old saying 'What you give is what you get'. Gratitude is *giving* thanks and we are then open to *receiving*. When we are ungrateful we are *taking* things for granted. We are then unintentionally taking from ourselves. We are holding back and limiting the Universal flow. Of course, we are not often aware of this, but with awareness we can change things. The magic words are '**Thank you'**. Thank you is the link from where you are now to where you want to be.

Your gratitude and your 'thank you' need to come from your heart. You need to *feel* this. The more you can feel it, the better it is. You will notice the difference.

Count your blessings

You may have heard people say, 'count your blessings' and that is exactly what you are doing when you think about all the things you are grateful for. Even being grateful for the smallest things in your life will make a difference to your vibration. When you vibrate at a higher level, you also attract people, things and circumstances at a higher level.

Scientists have also found that grateful people:[9]

- Show higher levels of positive emotions, life satisfaction, vitality and optimism.
- Experience lower levels of depression and stress.
- Have more capacity for compassion.
- Are more generous and helpful.
- Are more likely to have a spiritual practice.
- Place less importance on materialism.
- Are more likely to make progress towards important personal goals.
- Exercise more regularly, report fewer physical symptoms and feel healthier.

Here are a few things that I find work well:

Gratitude journal

I have kept a gratitude journal for many years. I write in it regularly, often every day, sometimes less often, but I always come back to it and I also love reading my gratitude lists from previous days, months or years. It is very uplifting.

Write down a few things that you are grateful for at least once a week. According to research by Professor Robert A. Emmons, University of California, those who kept gratitude journals on a weekly basis exercise more regularly, report fewer health problems, feel better about their lives as a whole, and are more optimistic about the upcoming week and about the future.[9]

Daily blessings

At the end of the day, before you fall asleep, reflect on the day and identify five things you are grateful for. Think about why you are grateful for each blessing. You can write it down in your journal if you like. Add 'thank you' at the end of each thing you are grateful for.

A few months ago, I lost my Aunt Elsa. She was so dear to me and a beacon of light throughout my life, so I was very sad when she passed away. When you lose someone dear, it makes you stop and really reflect on life. I felt great gratitude for having so many wonderful memories with my aunt, for all our conversations, our meetings and our sharing. I felt that every moment is so precious. Be grateful for your life, for each moment and for all the people you encounter.

Gratitude mirror

Years ago, when I realized that if I wanted to change my life for the better, I could not do that by only trying to fix all the problems on the outside but by looking within and changing myself. It wasn't other people's fault, the economy or anything else. It was up to me.

This is where the gratitude mirror comes in.

Go to a mirror and look directly at the person in the mirror and say out loud 'Thank you' with all your heart. Say thank you for being you. Be grateful for you, just as you are. Be grateful for the beautiful person in the mirror. If you find that it is difficult to say, 'thank you', just think the words. If you want to take this a step further, say three things about yourself that you are grateful for.

When you are grateful for yourself you move away from blame and self-criticism. If it helps, imagine that you are an angel looking down at yourself and all you see is beauty. Feel love and compassion for yourself. You are doing the best that you can. We are all going through difficulties, self-doubt and other challenges. Be kind to yourself and be grateful for having been given the gift of life.

Thank others

As I have been writing this chapter on gratitude, I have increased my own gratitude practice. One thing that I did today was to be extra friendly and grateful to all the people I encountered in the shops I was visiting. It is funny how well that works as I had excellent and friendly service in all the shops. Just having an attitude of gratitude helps!

Think about how you can show gratitude to the people you meet each day. It can be your work colleagues, shop or restaurant staff, someone on the phone or via email. Express how grateful you are in an easy and natural way and it will be much appreciated.

Are you expressing your gratitude to your loved ones? Include them in your gratitude practice. Tell them how much you appreciate them and what they do. It makes such a huge difference.

Find photos of the closest people in your life. With the photo in front of you, write down three things that you are grateful for about each person.

Be grateful for challenges

When we experience grief, sadness, disappointment and other similar feelings, it can be a real challenge. I know that this is difficult but if you can, try to get underneath these feelings and look at the seeds that are there. What do I mean by 'seeds'? There is always something of value in any experience, maybe even more so in the difficult experiences we have. Pain is an opportunity to become more aware and can be a blessing in disguise!

A few years ago, I had a small business selling a (Swedish) natural health product. I was responsible for introducing this product to the UK market. The product itself was wonderful but there were huge problems with the company that designed and were manufacturing this product. I found it difficult to work with the people in the company and was under increasing stress. I put in a huge amount of time but received very little gratitude. Then I started to receive threats and verbal abuse from someone within the company. I realized that, as much as I loved the product, I had to leave. I realized that the experience I was having with this company was pointing me in a different direction. The underlying message was that I needed to focus more on my own (yoga and health) business and only work with people who appreciated and respected me and my work. I also learnt a huge amount about business and marketing, which has been useful in the work I do today. So even though this experience was very stressful, I am grateful for what I learnt. It clearly pointed me in a different direction!

Forgiveness

The act of forgiveness is a truly transformational process. To forgive any person or situation that has caused you pain is to release them and yourself. By hanging on to old negative thoughts and emotions you only hurt yourself. It has been said that when you are unwilling to forgive someone, it is like drinking poison and waiting for the *other* person to get sick! So, let go of old hurt and bless the other person or situation. Wish them well and move on.

When you forgive someone, you take your power back. Unforgiveness takes a lot of energy and you don't want to spend a lot of time in that state. When we don't find a way to become harmonious with the things that cause us to suffer they become mental/emotional wounds and we carry them with us in our body and energy field.

When we *truly* forgive someone, all the negative thoughts and emotions disappear, and we have a sense of deep peace. The only feeling that is left is gratitude. You know that you have fully forgiven when you feel this peace and gratitude in your heart.

> *Forgiveness is the path to happiness.*
> *Do you want peace? Forgiveness offers it.*
> *Do you want happiness, a quiet mind, a certainty*
> *of purpose, and a sense of worth and beauty that*
> *transcends the world?*
> *Do you want care and safety, and the warmth of sure*
> *protection always?*
> *Do you want a quietness that cannot be disturbed,*
> *a gentleness that never can be hurt, a deep abiding*
> *comfort, and a rest so perfect it can never be upset?*
> *All this forgiveness offers you, and more.*
> *It sparkles on your eyes as you awake, and gives you joy*
> *with which to meet the day.*
> *It soothes your forehead while you sleep, and rests upon*
> *your eyelids so you see no dreams of fear and evil, malice*
> *and attack.*
> *And when you wake again, it offers you another day of*
> *happiness and peace.*
> *All this forgiveness offers you, and more.*
> **Self-forgiveness, A Course in Miracles, W-122.1–3[10]**

We are often so hard on ourselves. Everyone makes mistakes – yes even Buddha and Mother Theresa made mistakes! It is important to acknowledge when you have made a mistake, understand what you can learn from it, forgive yourself and move on. You don't want to hang on to the event and run it over and over in your head creating excessive guilt and needless suffering. This just leads to low self-confidence and even self-hatred.

Remind yourself that the mistake you have made is in the past and not the present. Remember that by blaming yourself, you are not helping yourself or anyone else. What we might do is to say, 'In the past, I had done or been xyz, and now I am (*connect with a positive intention*).' For example, 'In the past I made a mistake at work, but today I am doing things right and I feel positive about myself, my work and the future.'

The most important forgiveness is self-forgiveness. There is actually no other forgiveness! Even if you forgive another person it is only ever about yourself. You are the one letting go of the person or event. It is you who experience the peace and the healing. It is about releasing ourselves so that we can move forwards and say yes to life.

Reflection: Letter of forgiveness

One way of working with forgiveness – both of yourself and other people – is to write a letter.

1. Write a letter to a person either offering someone your forgiveness or asking for it from them. The person can be alive or dead. Then do a cleansing practice (in the next step).

2. Take the letter to a place where it is safe to burn it. Watch the fire consume the words that you have written and know that everything you have said is being absorbed by the Universe. Let the fire take away the pain. You can also shred it.

3. Give yourself time and space to be with the emotional release that often happens when you do this.

4. Then take the opportunity to write down a list of positive aspects about your life right now.

It is very powerful to write a letter to yourself asking for your own forgiveness or giving yourself forgiveness and then burn it. Follow the steps above.

Chapter 12
Spiritual Practice

'Spiritual practice is not just sitting and meditation. Practice is looking, thinking, touching, drinking, eating and talking. Every act, every breath, and every step can be practice and can help us to become more ourselves.'
Thich Nhat Hanh

So far we have explored many ways of bringing the Miracle of Yes into your life. All the things that we have talked about in previous chapters can come under the heading 'spiritual practice'. You can say yes to life by practising meditation, affirmations, gratitude, becoming aware of your thoughts and feelings, letting go of negative beliefs and so on. In this chapter, however, I am giving you a few more ideas of how to create a spiritual practice.

A spiritual practice or discipline is the regular performance of actions and activities undertaken for the purpose of cultivating spiritual development. To put it more simply a spiritual practice is a regular practice that draws you deeper into who you really are and helps you to connect with your True Self. Spiritual practices are not activities to add to your busy schedule or already crowded 'to do' list. They are not confined to a special place or time. They are what you do every day and a way of waking up to the spiritual reality all around you.

Why we need a spiritual practice

Oprah Winfrey says, 'There is no full life, no fulfilled or meaningful, sustainably joyful life without a connection to the spirit,' because a spiritual practice:
- Connects us with spirit/God/the Universe.
- Keeps us connected to our soul, to our real or True Self.
- Brings love, gratitude, joy, inner peace, guidance, energy and even bliss.
- Creates a sense of being 'grounded' and present in the now and in our heart.
- Helps us feel calmer, freer, and more relaxed and supported.
- Creates clarity and focus.
- Keeps you connected to the present moment.

When you were born you came in with a beautiful spiritual connection, but later you were unplugged from this Divine source. You were sent into a new physical reality and that is when your ego was born.

If you use your mobile phone all day, your battery will run down and you will get a warning message about charging it. If you ignore the message, your mobile will stop working and you won't be able to call anyone or connect to the Internet. In a similar way when we grow up, instead of being taught to develop our connection to the Divine, we are encouraged to unplug from this connection. We simply forget who we are and may live unfulfilled lives in fear of being unloved, unaccepted, rejected and disconnected. We become easily controlled and may try to control others.

The fear of this Divine power and wisdom can disconnect us from the source causing us to disconnect from our True Self. This often happens without us even realizing it. With an established, regular spiritual practice, you can 'switch on' again and reconnect with the Divine source and your True Self.

Many years ago, when I was studying healing, our teacher used to say that spiritual practice was a way of 'plugging in', and this is why spiritual practice is so important. It is not about feeling good and escaping reality for a little while, but about really finding and connecting with the Divine source. When we do this, everything changes, and we start to live from a deep and authentic place.

The spiritual teacher, mystic and mantra master Muz Murray speaks wisely on spiritual practice. He says that 'spiritual practice is something that needs to happen throughout the day, not just when you sit in meditation'. I totally agree. If you think that we are all one big energy field, then whatever you do minute to minute will either strengthen or weaken your connection with this field or the Divine/True Self. Whether you are chanting mantras, doing yoga or cleaning the house – it can all be spiritual practice. A spiritual practice can permeate everything you do. You *live* your spiritual practice.

Reflection: Your spiritual life

- Take a double page in your journal and write at the top, 'My spiritual life'. This is about creating your own version of spirituality.
- Write down whatever comes up. Don't limit yourself – be free and playful!

This is what I came up with:

Meditation, stillness, silence, creativity, candles, forest, breathing, bliss, centred, connection, yoga, nature, sea, wildlife, peace, joy, purple, friendship, darkness, light, Universe, galaxies, eternity, awakening, letting go, acceptance, forgiveness, gratitude, self-love, relaxation, clarity, sky, music, art.

Now it is your turn.

Creating a spiritual practice

A spiritual practice is something that makes you evolve. It can feel blissful and wonderful or, sometimes, a bit challenging. But it creates a foundation in your life and is something that you come back to, over and over again. It will be an important part of your life and over time you will notice a real difference to how you feel on a daily basis. You may want to try out several different practices before you find one that suits you. I think that it is important to stick with one practice for some time, to really experience the effects and benefits of it, before moving on to the next. Once you have tried out a few practices you will know what works for you.

My own spiritual practice is a yoga posture practice in the morning followed by 20-30 min seated meditation. I also go for a 1 hour silent walk in nature most days. About once a week I write in my journal and this will be a combination of a gratitude list, setting intentions, prayer and generally how I feel. I find that this provides an anchor in my day and week and gives me the space to maintain the connection with my True Self. This is *very* important to me.

We explored two spiritual practices, forgiveness and gratitude, in the previous chapter, but there are some other spiritual practices that can help you to maintain your connection with the Divine/your True Self.

Meditation

For me the most obvious spiritual practice is meditation. In Chapter 9, I outlined what meditation is and how to get started. Anyone can find 10-20 minutes each day to meditate and this is a wonderful investment in yourself, your wellbeing and sanity. Meditation is what most people think of when they think of a spiritual practice because it is about taking your awareness deeper into yourself and letting go of your busy mind. However, it is important to remember that you are not trying to reach a specific state or end result with meditation but just resting in what is. We are often far too eager to aim for some sort of goal, as this is how we have been conditioned to think and act. Find a good meditation practice, stick with it and relax into it.

Prayer

Most people think of prayers as something you do in church, but prayer is so much more than that. It is a way of communicating with the Universe and does not have to be linked to any formal religion. Did you know that four out of five people in the UK believe in prayer? And in the US over 80 per cent! I have spontaneously prayed many times for different things, admittedly often during difficult times!

Prayer has a similar effect on the body/mind as meditation. It lowers your blood pressure, it calms your mind and has many other benefits. Larry Dossey MD has written many books on this subject. When he first wanted to publish a book on the power of prayers in the 1980s his publisher refused to publish it as they found it too controversial (even with science to back up the astonishing effects of prayer). How times have changed! He eventually found another publisher and the book ended up being a *New York Times* bestseller.

The spiritual teacher Swami Chidanand Saraswati says, 'Prayer is like coming home. Just close your eyes and connect. That's it.' Absolutely. It couldn't be simpler. We don't need to remember long prayers or pray in a certain way. We just need to stop, relax and pray in a way that is natural and spontaneous. Tosha Silver in her wonderful book *Change Me Prayers* writes, 'The essence of prayer is surrender. You are inviting the Divine to make the changes IT wishes to make.'

So, we don't pray for a specific outcome, but rather hand over to the Divine and trust. And here is a beautiful prayer from her book:

Change me Divine Beloved into one who wants what You want for me. Let me trust that my needs will always be met in the Highest way when I allow You to guide me.

Reflection: Prayers

You can create a prayer for any area of your life – self-confidence, relationships, finance, health etc. – just be creative and spontaneous! The main thing is that it comes from your heart. Why not write down a prayer in your journal right now?

Letting go

Another powerful spiritual practice is to be *very* aware of your mind and your thoughts. When you encounter a situation where you feel angry, hurt or disappointed, take a step back, look at the situation, take a deep breath and let it go. You don't allow yourself to get involved and dragged into the situation but instead just let it pass, and it will pass! In other words, don't waste time and energy on negative conversations or situations. You still live your normal life, but you have the right to choose not to go down the path of arguments, anger and negativity. You become aware in every moment of your life what your mind is doing, and you move away from the tendency of the mind to amplify, exaggerate and scare you. You move away from the noise of the mind and you reside in a sea of peace. We are all seeking this state of peace, stillness and happiness and you can live a life like that by developing your awareness.

Letting go gives you the freedom you want. Freedom from mental/ emotional dramas. We let go of attachments and it moves us into the present moment. Your health and wellbeing will greatly benefit as a result. We become more spontaneous instead of rigidly sticking to plans and life becomes more fun.

Some people fall into the trap of needing to be in control of everything all of the time, however it is not possible. Can you control the train that is late, the computer that crashes or the friend that cancels your lunch date? Life is full of uncontrollable events such as these and we love certainty, so we struggle when things 'go wrong'. We want to feel safe and secure and we want to know where we are heading and what to expect in every moment. We want complete control of our lives. When things don't go to plan we get frustrated, angry and upset, and this makes it worse.

A couple of things that can help you to let go:

- **'I let go and surrender'**: Say this mantra out loud whenever you need to let go. You can direct the mantra to anywhere in your body where you feel that you are holding on, and the mantra will help you to release. You are talking to your True Self and you are creating an energetic response and more space in your mind. You can also use this mantra silently in your meditation, especially if you have a hard time letting go.
- **Offer it to the Universe**: Whatever you are trying to control, offer it to the Universe. You can say, 'Thank you for helping me to let go of this. Thank you for taking this from me.' Know that it has gone to a higher place and will be transformed into something better. Observe if any new ideas or solutions come up after this practice.

Spending time alone

Often, we want to fill up every part of the day with some sort of activity, as we are subconsciously scared of being on our own or of going deeper. It is a good spiritual practice to sometimes allow ourselves to spend time alone and in silence with nothing to do. In that 'empty' space, you get to know yourself better and it is from that stillness and space that a new understanding can emerge. It is nothing to be fearful of, because we will all sooner or later encounter this 'empty' space, and it is good to be friends with it. Personally, I love having times of 'emptiness' as I can then allow everything that wants to flow through me to do so, without interruptions of all the activities of the day.

Yoga

Many people think that yoga is an exercise class, but this couldn't be further from the truth. Yoga is a spiritual practice. In fact, it is one of the oldest spiritual practices in history as it goes back more than 5,000 years. We talked about embodiment in Chapter 4 and Hatha Yoga is the ultimate embodiment practice. We can also call it a moving meditation. But apart from the physical aspect of yoga, there is a multitude of different spiritual practices within the yoga tradition. For example, if we look at the eight limbs of yoga, asana (yoga postures) is only one limb. The other seven limbs have to do with things such as non-violence, truthfulness, purity of mind, acceptance, self-study, breathing, cleansing practices, stilling the mind, etc.

The sage Patanjali's definition of yoga in the *Yoga Sutras* (1.2) is 'Yoga is the stilling, or restraint, of the fluctuations of the mind.'

So where do you start with yoga as a spiritual practice? My advice is to use the yoga postures as you normally would, but be *fully* present. Make your yoga posture practice into a beautiful spiritual practice. Work on coordinating your breath *exactly* with each movement and keep the movement and breath slow and steady. Really *feel* each movement/posture. Be *aware* of sensations anywhere in your body and be aware of your thoughts and feelings as you do your practice. You will notice with time that your thoughts will subside as you practice yoga.

Nature

Ever since I was a little girl I have loved spending time in nature. I think it is because I have always felt very much at home there and know nature is a powerful healer. When you spend time in nature your heart opens naturally. You don't have to *try* to open your heart, it just happens by itself. Your mental chatter slows down and you open to the wonders around you. You effortlessly connect with the trees, flowers, plants, rocks, water, sky, sunshine, air. Time in nature connects you to spirit, the earth and the Universe.

When you spend time in nature, try to really *be* there – fully and completely. Really look at everything around you. Notice the shapes, colours, sounds, textures. Take your time and enjoy. You can also practice gratitude while being in nature. Feeling gratitude for everything around you and saying, 'thank you' several times.

Creativity

In Chapter 5 we looked at activities that made time 'disappear', i.e. you are so fully involved in something that you forget about time. This often happens when we do something creative such as painting, photography, craft, woodwork, gardening, dancing, writing or something that we really enjoy. When we have the feeling that everything else has just disappeared and we are totally focused and involved in what we are doing we are actually performing a spiritual practice. We have reached a 'still point' within, often referred to as 'flow'. Creativity is a powerful force that takes us out of our self-limitations. It can be a wonderful spiritual practice and make your life richer and more colourful.

Setting an intention

An intention is a way of directing your mind towards a purpose or quality. It is important that your intention comes from the heart. An intention can be likened to a seed. You sow a seed/intention in your mind and watch it grow. And then you let go. It can be a small or big intention and it is great to set an intention at the beginning of your meditation or yoga practice or at the start of your day or week. Often an intention is based around your values and perspectives. Here are a few examples:
- Find balance
- Open my mind and heart
- Peace
- Embrace change
- Give and receive love
- Connect with others
- Relaxation
- Love

Be aimless

Create an aimless day! This is a great spiritual practice! Be receptive to how your day wants to evolve without any planning or interference of the mind. Listen to your intuition. Where do you want to go today? What do you want to do? Allow your intuition to take over for a few hours.

For example: Go out for a walk, and just allow your intuition to lead you. Or take the car to a place you've never been before or a train ride to somewhere new. Try a new café or restaurant. Or maybe sit on a bench and just let the world go by. Or try a practice, such as those organized by Todd Acamesis in London who runs what he calls 'synchronicity walks'. A group of people meet up somewhere and then use a dice to decide which direction to go. They let the dice and their intuition lead them and they end up in the most unbelievable and exciting places and situations.

I often go for aimless walks with my camera. I often find little roads and paths I have never been on before, and I often discover delightful things and scenery! This is great fun and makes you feel alive and adventurous!

Conclusion

The Journey

'To know yourself as the Being underneath the thinker,
The stillness underneath the mental noise,
The love and joy underneath the pain,
Is freedom, salvation, enlightenment.'
Eckhart Tolle

It was my own journey and learning process that took me to the point of writing this book. All the different situations I have encountered, the places I have lived and visited, the people I have met and all the experiences I have had, took me to this moment. In a way, I am not any of those experiences. I am not my past. I am not what other people think I am, or even what I myself think I am! But all those experiences shaped me in a certain way and made it possible for me to arrive at this moment. I love this learning process that life is. The good, the bad, the ups and downs. And I am excited about the next step on the journey.

The title of this book, *The Miracle of Yes,* came from deep within me. I didn't have to think about it. It just arrived one day. And this is what can happen when you live your life in the 'Yes Flow'. You have largely bypassed the interruptive, over-active and confusing mind ('no') and answers, solutions, ideas and inspiration ('yes') flow through you freely. This saves time and energy and make life easier and more fun. And this is available to *everyone*!

Try to imagine a world where everyone is heart-based and has let go of all negativity. A world where everyone is free and lives in harmony and balance with everyone and everything around them. I don't know if we will ever, as the human race, reach this but I live in great hope. I believe that if we can all contribute a little to this by creating more peace within us, then there will be a tipping point when enough of us are in harmony, so that this balances out all the negativity on Earth.

It is easy to think that what we do on an individual basis has no effect. It is also very easy to think that what we do is just for ourselves and doesn't involve other people, but this is not so. Whatever we do has a profound effect – on ourselves, everyone around us and the planet.

We are all here to learn and, just as you would be gentle with a little child, you need to be gentle with yourself on this learning journey. You don't have to learn everything in one go. Work step by step and focus on the things that you are drawn to most. For some people, it could be mantra and for others it might be some of the exercises (*Reflections*) in this book. Or it could be working with the shadow, forgiveness or breathwork. We all have our own individual path to saying 'yes' to the miracle of life.

I want to conclude by expressing a huge thank you to you, the reader, from my heart. Good luck on your journey. And please do contact me to let me know how you are getting on. I would love to know.

Namaste.

References

1. The UCLA Loneliness Scale was developed to assess subjective feelings of loneliness or social isolation. Items for the original version of the scale were based on statements used by lonely individuals to describe feelings of loneliness (Russell, Peplau, & Ferguson, 1978). Jaremka, L., *et al.* 'Loneliness promotes inflammation during acute stress', *Psychol Sci.*, 2013 Jul; 1;24(7):1089-97. doi: 10.1177/0956797612464059. Epub 2013 Apr 29.

2. Popp, F. *et al.*, 'Mechanism of interaction between electromagnetic fields and living organism', *Science in China*, 2000; (Series C), no 2 (2000): 207–18.

3. Armour, J. *et al, Neurocardiology: Anatomical and Functional Principles* (Montreal University, 1991)

4. McCraty, R. HeartMath Research Centre, Science of the Heart

5. Vedanta is one of the world's most ancient spiritual philosophies, based on the Vedas, the sacred scriptures of India and one of the six orthodox schools of Hindu philosophy. Vedanta literally means 'end of the Vedas', reflecting ideas that emerged from the speculations and philosophies contained in the Upanishads

6. Sat Bir Singh Khalsa, PhD, assistant professor and researcher in the field of body mind medicine at Harvard Medical School

7. https://www.ncbi.nlm.nih.gov/pmc/articles/PMC3004979/

8. https://www.ucdavis.edu/news/mindfulness-meditation-associated-lower-stress-hormone

9. https://www.ncbi.nlm.nih.gov/pubmed/12585811

10. A Course in Miracles: Lessons with a transformational curriculum in Self-realization, through Love and forgiveness

Further Resources

Events and coaching

Why not join one of my YES weekends or day workshops in Kent where I work with small groups? These events are covering a lot of what I have written about in this book. The focus is on YES – Yoga, Empowerment, Spirituality and these events are deeply relaxing and inspirational. Or why not join one of my Yoga and Meditation Retreats in beautiful locations abroad?

I also offer private sessions in Kent or via Skype. These are healing sessions, where we can explore any issues to identify the root cause and reasons why you may be struggling. With more than 30 years' experience of astrology, I also incorporate astrology in the session. We also look at your thought patterns, beliefs, emotions, energy and much more to help you gain insight and ultimately understand yourself better.

Websites:

You will find further resources including information about events and courses, and recorded guided meditations on:

www.rosemariesorokin.com
www.innerlightyoga.co.uk
www.yogapilatesholidays.com

Join me on social media:
Facebook: @rosemariesorokinauthorandcoach
Facebook: @innerlightyogaandhealthco
Twitter: @innerlightrose
Instagram: @innerlightyogaandhealth

Suggested Reading

Adyashanti, *The End of Your World;*
——————–, *Falling into Grace*
Braden, Gregg, *Resilience from the Heart*
——————–, *The Turning Point*
——————–, *Human by Design*
——————–, *The Spontaneous Healing of Beliefs*
Catto, Jamie, *Insanely Gifted*
Davidji, *Secrets of Meditation*
Ford, Debbie, *The Dark Side of the Light Chasers*
Filmer-Lorch, Alexander, *Inside Meditation*
————————, *The Inner Power of Stillness*
Gangaji, *The Diamond in Your Pocket*
Hay, Louise, *You Can Heal Your Life*
——————–, *Heal Your Body*
——————–, *The Power is Within You*
Holden, Robert, *Loveability*
——————–, *Holy Shift*
——————–, *Shift Happens*
Moorjani, Anita, *Dying to Be Me*
——————–, *What if This is Heaven?*
Ray, Reginald, *Touching Enlightenment: Finding Realization in the Body*
Schucman, Helen, *A Course in Miracles*
Singer, Michael, *The Untethered Soul*
Tolle, Eckhart, *The Power of Now*
——————–, *A New Earth*
——————–, *Stillness Speaks*
Williams, Nick, *The Work You Were Born to Do*
——————–, *Powerful Beyond Measure*
——————–, *How to be Inspired*
——————–, *Resisting Your Soul*
——————–, *The Business You Were Born to Create*
Swan, Teal, *Shadows before Dawn*
Silver, Tosha, *Change Me Prayers*
Vitale, Joe, *Expect Miracles*
——, *Zero Limits*
——————–, *The Attractor Factor*
Walsch, Neale Donald, *The Only Thing That Matters*

Printed in Great Britain
by Amazon